Common Core Mastery

Reading Paired Text

Grade **3**

The following images were provided through Shutterstock.com and are protected by copyright:
Marco Uliana (page 96), Decha Thapanya (page 96), Maslov Dmitry (page 97), Merkushev Vasiliy (page 117), Cheryl Casey (page 156), charobnica (pages 164–165)

Permissions for the remaining images were provided by the organizations and individuals listed below:
Currier & Ives (page 36), Giuseppe Bertini (page 136)

Editorial Development: Lisa Vitarisi Mathews
Kathleen Wendell
Writing: Barbara Allman
Renee Biermann
Kira Freed
Camille Liscinsky
Guadalupe Lopez
Carol Pecot
Teera Safi
Anastasia Scopelitis
Kathleen Wendell
Copy Editing: Laurie Westrich
Art Direction: Cheryl Puckett
Cover Design: Yuki Meyer
Cover Illustration: Chris Vallo
Illustration: Len Borozinski
Judith Cummins
Design/Production: Susan Lovell
Jessica Onken

EMC 1373

Evan-Moor.
Helping Children Learn

Visit
teaching-standards.com
to view a correlation
of this book.
This is a free service.

Correlated to State and
Common Core State Standards

For information about other Evan-Moor products, call 1-800-777-4362, fax 1-800-777-4332, or visit our Web site, www.evan-moor.com.
Entire contents © 2014 EVAN-MOOR CORP.
18 Lower Ragsdale Drive, Monterey, CA 93940-5746. Printed in USA.

CPSIA: Printed by McNaughton & Gunn, Saline, MI USA. [12/2013]

Contents

Introduction

Social Studies Units

The Value of Volunteering 13

Essential Question: What can citizens do to help each other?

A Place to Call Home 33

Essential Question: How do people decide where to live?

Meeting the Father of a Country 53

Essential Question: What was the first United States president like?

Picturing the World 73

Essential Question: How did we figure out what our world looks like?

Science Units

Corrections
Common Core State Standards

RIT — Reading Standards for Informational Text, Grade 3	Social Studies Selections							
	Volunteer Your Time	Victory Dance	Why Live Near a River?	New Land, New Life	The Generals and Their Dogs	The Legend of the Cherry Tree	Putting the Pieces Together	The Edge of the World
Key Ideas and Details								
3.1 Ask and answer questions to demonstrate understanding of a text, referring explicitly to the text as the basis for the answers.	•		•		•		•	
3.2 Determine the main idea of a text; recount the key details and explain how they support the main idea.	•		•		•		•	
3.3 With prompting and support, describe the connection between two individuals, events, ideas, or pieces of information in a text.	•		•		•		•	
Craft and Structure								
3.4 Determine the meaning of general academic and domain-specific words and phrases in a text relevant to a grade 3 topic or subject area.	•		•		•		•	
3.5 Use text features and search tools (e.g., key words, sidebars, hyperlinks) to locate information relevant to a given topic efficiently.	•		•		•		•	
3.6 Distinguish their own point of view from that of the author of a text.			•					
Integration of Knowledge and Ideas								
3.7 Use information gained from illustrations (e.g., maps, photographs) and the words in a text to demonstrate understanding of the text (e.g., where, when, why, and how key events occur).			•				•	
3.8 Describe the logical connection between particular sentences and paragraphs in a text (e.g., comparison, cause/effect, first/second/third in a sequence).			•					
Range of Reading and Level of Text Complexity								
3.10 By the end of the year, read and comprehend informational texts, including history/social studies, science, and technical texts, at the high end of the grades 2–3 text complexity band independently and proficiently.	•		•		•		•	

Reading Paired Text • EMC 1373 • © Evan-Moor Corp.

Correlations
Common Core State Standards

Science Selections								RIT — Reading Standards for Informational Text, Grade 3
Meat-Eating Plants	The Tiger and the Jackals	Water All Around Us	Panika's Favorite Season	New Invention, New Universe	SpaceBook Friends	Growing with Gravity	Lean Green Beans	
Key Ideas and Details								
•		•		•		•		**3.1** Ask and answer questions to demonstrate understanding of a text, referring explicitly to the text as the basis for the answers.
•		•		•		•		**3.2** Determine the main idea of a text; recount the key details and explain how they support the main idea.
•		•		•		•		**3.3** With prompting and support, describe the connection between two individuals, events, ideas, or pieces of information in a text.
Craft and Structure								
•		•		•		•		**3.4** Determine the meaning of general academic and domain-specific words and phrases in a text relevant to a grade 3 topic or subject area.
•		•		•		•		**3.5** Use text features and search tools (e.g., key words, sidebars, hyperlinks) to locate information relevant to a given topic efficiently.
				•				**3.6** Distinguish their own point of view from that of the author of a text.
Integration of Knowledge and Ideas								
				•				**3.7** Use information gained from illustrations (e.g., maps, photographs) and the words in a text to demonstrate understanding of the text (e.g., where, when, why, and how key events occur).
		•		•		•		**3.8** Describe the logical connection between particular sentences and paragraphs in a text (e.g., comparison, cause/effect, first/second/third in a sequence).
Range of Reading and Level of Text Complexity								
•		•		•		•		**3.10** By the end of the year, read and comprehend informational texts, including history/social studies, science, and technical texts, at the high end of the grades 2–3 text complexity band independently and proficiently.

Corrections
Common Core State Standards

	Social Studies Selections							
RL Reading Standards for Literature, Grade 3	Volunteer Your Time	Victory Dance	Why Live Near a River?	New Land, New Life	The Generals and Their Dogs	The Legend of the Cherry Tree	Putting the Pieces Together	The Edge of the World
Key Ideas and Details								
3.1 Ask and answer questions to demonstrate understanding of a text, referring explicitly to the text as the basis for the answers.		●		●		●		●
3.2 Recount stories, including fables, folktales, and myths from diverse cultures; determine the central message, lesson, or moral and explain how it is conveyed through key details in the text.		●		●		●		●
3.3 Describe characters in a story (e.g., their traits, motivations, or feelings) and explain how their actions contribute to the sequence of events.		●		●		●		●
Craft and Structure								
3.4 Determine the meaning of words and phrases as they are used in a text, distinguishing literal from nonliteral language.		●		●		●		●
3.6 Distinguish their own point of view from that of the narrator or those of the characters.		●		●		●		●
Integration of Knowledge and Ideas								
3.7 Explain how specific aspects of a text's illustrations contribute to what is conveyed by the words in a story (e.g., create mood, emphasize aspects of a character or setting).		●						
Range of Reading and Level of Text Complexity								
3.10 By the end of the year, read and comprehend literature, including stories, dramas, and poetry, at the high end of the grades 2–3 text complexity band independently and proficiently.		●		●		●		●

W Writing Standards, Grade 3								
Text Types and Purposes								
3.1 Write opinion pieces on topics or texts, supporting a point of view with reasons.			●					
3.2 Write informative/explanatory texts to examine a topic and convey ideas and information clearly.	●	●		●	●	●	●	●

Correlations
Common Core State Standards

Science Selections								RL — Reading Standards for Literature, Grade 3
Meat-Eating Plants	The Tiger and the Jackals	Water All Around Us	Panika's Favorite Season	New Invention, New Universe	SpaceBook Friends	Growing with Gravity	Lean Green Beans	
								Key Ideas and Details
	●		●		●		●	**3.1** Ask and answer questions to demonstrate understanding of a text, referring explicitly to the text as the basis for the answers.
	●		●		●		●	**3.2** Recount stories, including fables, folktales, and myths from diverse cultures; determine the central message, lesson, or moral and explain how it is conveyed through key details in the text.
	●		●		●			**3.3** Describe characters in a story (e.g., their traits, motivations, or feelings) and explain how their actions contribute to the sequence of events.
								Craft and Structure
	●		●		●		●	**3.4** Determine the meaning of words and phrases as they are used in a text, distinguishing literal from nonliteral language.
					●		●	**3.6** Distinguish their own point of view from that of the narrator or those of the characters.
								Integration of Knowledge and Ideas
	●				●		●	**3.7** Explain how specific aspects of a text's illustrations contribute to what is conveyed by the words in a story (e.g., create mood, emphasize aspects of a character or setting).
								Range of Reading and Level of Text Complexity
	●		●		●		●	**3.10** By the end of the year, read and comprehend literature, including stories, dramas, and poetry, at the high end of the grades 2–3 text complexity band independently and proficiently.

								W — Writing Standards, Grade 3
								Text Types and Purposes
				● (unit prompt)				**3.1** Write opinion pieces on topics or texts, supporting a point of view with reasons.
●	●	●	●	●	●	●	●	**3.2** Write informative/explanatory texts to examine a topic and convey ideas and information clearly.

Correlations
Texas Essential Knowledge and Skills

110.14. English Language Arts and Reading, Grade 3	Social Studies Selections					
	Volunteer Your Time	Victory Dance	Why Live Near a River?	New Land, New Life	The Generals and Their Dogs	The Legend of the Cherry Tree
Reading						
(4B) Vocabulary Development. Students understand new vocabulary and use it when reading and writing. Students are expected to use context to determine the relevant meaning of unfamiliar words or distinguish among multiple meaning words and homographs.	●	●	●	●	●	●
(6) Comprehension of Literary Text/Poetry. Students understand, make inferences, and draw conclusions about the structure and elements of poetry and provide evidence from text to support their understanding. Students are expected to describe the characteristics of various forms of poetry and how they create imagery (e.g., narrative poetry, lyrical poetry, humorous poetry, free verse).						
(8B) Comprehension of Literary Text/Fiction. Students understand, make inferences, and draw conclusions about the structure and elements of fiction and provide evidence from text to support their understanding. Students are expected to describe the interaction of characters including their relationships and the changes they undergo.		●		●		●
(13A, B, D) Comprehension of Informational Text/Expository Text. Students analyze, make inferences and draw conclusions about expository text and provide evidence from text to support their understanding. Students are expected to identify the details or facts that support the main idea; draw conclusions from the facts presented in text and support those assertions with textual evidence; and use text features (e.g., bold print, captions, key words, italics) to locate information and make and verify predictions about contents of text.	●		●		●	
(13C) Comprehension of Informational Text/Expository Text. Students analyze, make inferences and draw conclusions about expository text and provide evidence from text to support their understanding. Students are expected to identify explicit cause and effect relationships among ideas in texts.			●			
Writing						
(17A) Writing Process. Students use elements of the writing process (planning, drafting, revising, editing, publishing) to compose text. Students are expected to plan a first draft by selecting a genre appropriate for conveying the intended meaning to an audience and generating ideas through a range of strategies (e.g., brainstorming, graphic organizers, logs, journals).	●	●	●	●	●	●
(20A, C) Expository/Procedural Texts. Students write expository and procedural or work-related texts to communicate ideas and information to specific audiences for specific purposes. Students are expected to create brief compositions that: i) establish a central idea in a topic sentence; ii) include supporting sentences with simple facts, details, and explanations; and write responses to literary or expository texts that demonstrate an understanding of the text.	●	●	●	●	●	●
(21) Persuasive Texts. Students write persuasive texts to influence the attitudes or actions of a specific audience on specific issues. Students are expected to write persuasive essays for appropriate audiences that establish a position and use supporting details.			●			

Reading Paired Text • EMC 1373 • © Evan-Moor Corp.

Correlations
Texas Essential Knowledge and Skills

	Science Selections									
	Putting the Pieces Together	The Edge of the World	Meat-Eating Plants	The Tiger and the Jackals	Water All Around Us	Panika's Favorite Season	New Invention, New Universe	SpaceBook Friends	Growing with Gravity	Lean Green Beans
	●	●	●	●	●	●	●	●	●	●
										●
		●		●		●		●		
	●		●		●		●		●	
	●		●		●		●		●	
	●	●	●	●	●	●	●	●	●	●
	●	●	●	●	●	●	●	●	●	●
								● (unit prompt)		

How to Use

Reading Paired Text contains reading selections about grade-level social studies and science topics. The supporting comprehension and writing activities use Common Core methodology to guide students to closely examine the texts, discuss the topic, and ultimately improve their reading comprehension. The pairing of texts allows students to compare multiple viewpoints and provides opportunities to integrate information.

Each unit contains two thematically related selections, an informational text and a literary text, that are focused around an essential question. Each selection's activities include vocabulary development in context, an oral close reading discussion, comprehension questions, and a writing prompt. The unit assessment includes discussion of the topic, texts, and essential question, as well as a writing prompt.

Unit Overview

The unit title, the topic-related student objective, and the essential question are presented.

TOPIC INTRODUCTION
Background information connects students to the topic without giving away the selection content.

PAIRED TEXT SELECTIONS
Under each selection, genre and Guided Reading Levels (L–P) are listed, as well as teacher pages and student activities.

ASSESSMENT MATERIALS
At the end of the unit are activities that help students compare and integrate what they have learned about the topic.

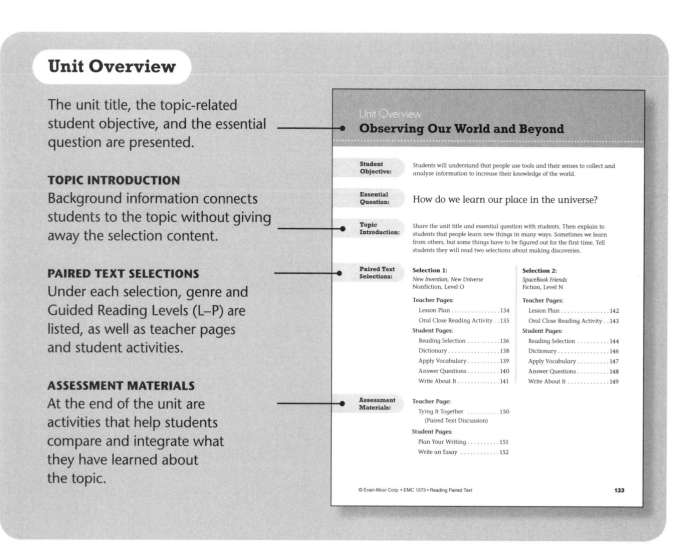

Unit Overview
Observing Our World and Beyond

Student Objective: Students will understand that people use tools and their senses to collect and analyze information to increase their knowledge of the world.

Essential Question: How do we learn our place in the universe?

Topic Introduction: Share the unit title and essential question with students. Then explain to students that people learn new things in many ways. Sometimes we learn from others, but some things have to be figured out for the first time. Tell students they will read two selections about making discoveries.

Paired Text Selections:

Selection 1:
New Invention, New Universe
Nonfiction, Level O

Teacher Pages:
Lesson Plan 134
Oral Close Reading Activity . .135
Student Pages:
Reading Selection 136
Dictionary 138
Apply Vocabulary 139
Answer Questions 140
Write About It 141

Selection 2:
SpaceBook Friends
Fiction, Level N

Teacher Pages:
Lesson Plan 142
Oral Close Reading Activity . .143
Student Pages:
Reading Selection 144
Dictionary 146
Apply Vocabulary 147
Answer Questions 148
Write About It 149

Assessment Materials:

Teacher Page:
Tying It Together 150
(Paired Text Discussion)
Student Pages:
Plan Your Writing 151
Write an Essay 152

© Evan-Moor Corp. • EMC 1373 • Reading Paired Text   **133**

Teacher Pages

LESSON PLAN

The suggested teaching path guides you through each selection and related activities. It also provides selection-related background information for students to access before reading.

ORAL CLOSE READING ACTIVITY

These classroom discussion questions focus on important details and help students use context clues and word analysis to figure out the meaning of unfamiliar words.

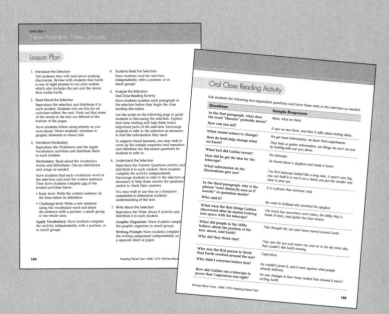

Student Pages

SELECTIONS

Students read two selections on the unit topic. The topics should be familiar to students from their social studies and science lessons. Selections focus on a specific aspect of the topic and may offer multiple viewpoints. The texts are often augmented with illustrations, photos, diagrams, other graphics, and additional vocabulary support.

DICTIONARY

Academic vocabulary words from the selection are defined and lines are provided for students to write a sentence using the word.

APPLY VOCABULARY

Students practice applying vocabulary by completing sentences with the appropriate vocabulary word.

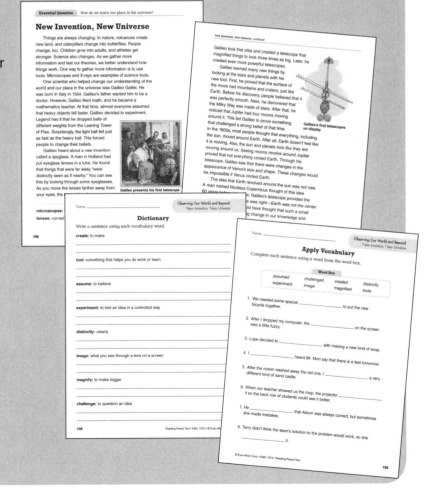

Student Pages, continued

ANSWER QUESTIONS

Students review key ideas of the selection by answering both literal and inferential questions.

WRITE ABOUT IT

Students further show what they have learned by writing. They arrange ideas and details in a graphic organizer, then respond to a text-based writing prompt.

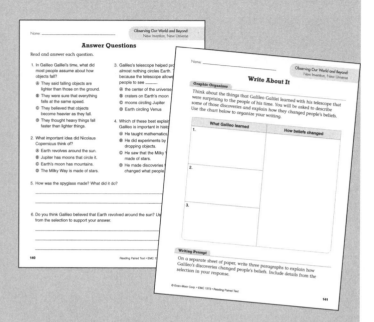

Assessment Materials

Teacher Page

TYING IT TOGETHER

Oral discussion questions tie together how both selections relate to the unit topic and the essential question.

Student Pages

PLAN YOUR WRITING,

WRITE AN ESSAY

Students arrange ideas and details from both selections in a graphic organizer, then respond to a topic-based writing prompt.

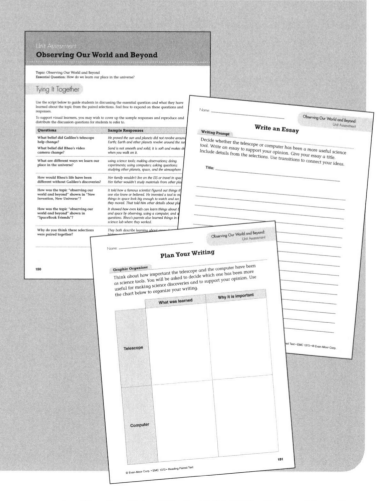

The Value of Volunteering

Student Objective:
Students will understand that many citizens volunteer their time to help others in their communities.

Essential Question:

What can citizens do to help each other?

Topic Introduction:
Share the unit title and essential question with students. Then explain that people help make their communities better places in which to live by helping each other. Tell students that they will read two selections about how citizens volunteer to help each other.

Paired Text Selections:

Assessment Materials:

Lesson Plan

1. Introduce the Selection

Tell students they will read information about how citizens volunteer to help their community. Discuss the meaning of the word *citizen* and explain that people who live in a community are called citizens. Then ask students if they have ever volunteered and invite them to share their experiences.

2. Read Aloud the Selection

Reproduce the selection and distribute it to each student. Students will use this for all activities within the unit. Point out that some of the words in the text are defined at the bottom of the pages.

Have students follow along silently as you read aloud. Direct students' attention to graphic elements or visual aids.

3. Introduce Vocabulary

Reproduce the Dictionary and the Apply Vocabulary activities and distribute them to each student.

Dictionary: Read aloud the vocabulary words and definitions. Point out that *bank* is a multiple-meaning word, or a homonym. Discuss definitions and usage as needed.

Have students find each vocabulary word in the selection and read the context sentence. Then have students complete <u>one</u> of the leveled activities below:

- Basic level: Write the context sentence on the lines below its definition.

- Challenge level: Write a new sentence using the vocabulary word and share the sentence with a partner, a small group, or the whole class.

Apply Vocabulary: Have students complete the activity independently, with a partner, or in small groups.

4. Students Read the Selection

Have students read the selection independently, with a partner, or in small groups.

5. Analyze the Selection: Oral Close Reading Activity

Have students number each paragraph in the selection before they begin the close reading discussion.

Use the script on the following page to guide students in discussing the selection. Explain that close reading will help them notice important parts of the selection. Encourage students to refer to the selection as necessary to find the information they need.

To support visual learners, you may wish to cover up the sample responses and reproduce and distribute the discussion questions for students to refer to.

6. Understand the Selection

Reproduce the Answer Questions activity and distribute it to each student. Have students complete the activity independently. Encourage students to refer to the selection as necessary to help them answer the questions and/or to check their answers.

You may wish to use this as a formative assessment to determine students' understanding of the text.

7. Write About the Selection

Reproduce the Write About It activity and distribute it to each student.

Graphic Organizer: Have students complete the graphic organizer in small groups.

Writing Prompt: Have students complete the writing assignment independently on a separate sheet of paper.

Oral Close Reading Activity

Ask students the following text-dependent questions and have them refer to the selection as needed.

Questions	Sample Responses
Does this story take place now or long ago?	*long ago*
How can you tell?	*It was when bison roamed the plains and when people started coming west in covered wagons.*
What have the elders decided?	*that the whole community should move west to the Snake River*
When did people come from Spain?	*when the elders were young*
What happened then?	*Many people became very sick.*
In the third paragraph, what does the word "skillful" probably mean?	*full of skill, able to do something well*
How did you figure it out?	*A skill is something you can do, and "ful" is a suffix meaning "full of."*
How does the tribe get food now?	*They hunt bison.*
What are salmon and bass?	*types of fish*
How did you figure it out?	*They are talking about relying on fish in the Snake River, which has a lot of salmon and bass.*
Why is eating trout a treat?	*They don't get to fish very much because the stream is far away.*
What is the dream about silver-colored fish a symbol of?	*the Snake River, the place she is moving to*
What is the dream about playing hide-and-seek a symbol of?	*the plains, the place she has lived all her life*
What chores will be easier after they move?	*the things that use water: carrying water to camp, cleaning their belongings, bathing*
In the last paragraph, what does "a piece of my heart will hide forever in the tall grasses" probably mean?	*The narrator will always love the plains.*

New Land, New Life

Last week, I learned we are moving. I am scared, since I have never traveled beyond the wide meadows. I feel sad because the Great Plains are the only home I know. My grandmother is also full of sorrow. She says when she came to the plains at my age, it was the happiest day of her life. But still, Grandmother agrees with our Shoshoni elders that it is time to travel to new ground.

On a dusky evening, the elders called the community to a meeting. They announced that we must prepare to move west to the Snake River. The elders declared that it was too dangerous for us to meet with the pioneers who were coming from the east in covered wagons. Our elders remember that many Shoshoni became very sick when they traded with the people from Spain. They do not want us to suffer like their parents did.

My father told my younger brother and me that we will rely on fish in our new home. Catfish, salmon, and bass will be plentiful in the Snake River, but there will be few, if any, bison roaming the land. This will be a big change for us hunters. The elders fear that the covered wagons will bring an end to the bison. We will have

plains: flat, grassy land with few trees

bison: large, fierce animals that used to roam on the plains

to become more skillful at fishing. The only fishing I do now is in the stream far beyond our camp. Right now, eating trout is a treat for us.

I went to sleep last night and dreamed of a stream so big that I could not see its other shore. I dreamed of hundreds of silver-colored fish leaping out of the water. I also dreamed of sun-filled afternoons playing hide-and-seek in the tall grasses with other girls. This is one of my favorite games to play. What will the other children and I do at the river?

This morning, I told my mother about my dreams. She said my friends and I will have much to explore. She also pointed out that many chores will be easier with a water source so close by. We will no longer have to carry water a long distance to our camp. We can wash our belongings at the river's edge. We can bathe our bodies in the flowing waterway. I then realized that I feel both sadness and excitement about our big journey. A piece of my heart will hide forever in the tall grasses. But maybe I will find happiness in my new life by the river, like my grandmother did on the plains.

Dictionary

Write a sentence using each vocabulary word.

elder: a wise older person

_____

_____

community: all the people who live in an area

_____

_____

declare: to state in a strong or official way

_____

_____

rely: to need, use, expect to have

_____

_____

plentiful: many, much, having plenty

_____

_____

source: a place to get something

_____

_____

distance: the amount of space between two places or things

_____

_____

Apply Vocabulary

Complete each sentence using a word from the word box.

Word Box

| community | declared | distance | elders |
| plentiful | rely | source | |

1. Our _____ have interesting stories to tell us about the past.

2. The library is a good _____ for books and magazines.

3. Our neighborhood school offers art classes to the whole _____.

4. There will be a _____ amount of blackberries this summer.

5. Baby snowy owls _____ on their parents to feed them.

6. The principal _____ today a snow day, so we got to stay home from school.

7. My home is a short _____ from the ball park.

Write two new sentences. Use a word from the word box in each.

1. _____

_____

2. _____

_____

Answer Questions

Read and answer each question.

1. Why is the narrator's family going to move?

   Ⓐ Bison are too hard to find.

   Ⓑ They are running out of food.

   Ⓒ Travelers might make them sick.

   Ⓓ People from Spain want their land.

2. In her new home, the narrator will have to _____.

   Ⓐ find more bison

   Ⓑ fish by the river

   Ⓒ meet people from the east

   Ⓓ play games in tall grass

3. How does the narrator's family use bison on the plains?

   Ⓐ They eat bison.

   Ⓑ They ride bison.

   Ⓒ The bison help them fish.

   Ⓓ The bison keep strangers away.

4. Why is the narrator afraid to move?

   Ⓐ She has never left the plains.

   Ⓑ She does not like eating fish.

   Ⓒ She will miss her brother.

   Ⓓ She had scary dreams.

5. How are the narrator and her grandmother alike? Use examples from the story to support your answer.

   _____

   _____

   _____

   _____

6. How does the narrator feel about her big move by the end of the story? Use examples from the story to support your answer.

   _____

   _____

   _____

   _____

Write About It

Graphic Organizer

Think about how the narrator's new and old homes are similar and different. You will be asked to compare the narrator's homes on the plains and on the Snake River. Use the chart below to organize your writing.

Similarities

Differences	
Home on the plains	**Home by the Snake River**

Writing Prompt

On a separate sheet of paper, write two paragraphs to compare the similarities and differences between the narrator's old home on the plains and new home by the river. Include details from the selection in your response.

A Place to Call Home

Topic: A Place to Call Home

Essential Question: How do people decide where to live?

Tying It Together

Use the script below to guide students in discussing the essential question and what they have learned about the topic from the paired selections. Feel free to expand on these questions and responses.

To support visual learners, you may wish to cover up the sample responses and reproduce and distribute the discussion questions for students to refer to.

Questions	Sample Responses
When the Shoshoni move to their new home along the Snake River, how might their lives change?	*They will eat more fish and less bison; it will be easier to do chores that use water and to get drinking water; their community could flood.*
Why were rivers so important in pioneer days?	*for drinking, cleaning, bathing without having to carry water far; for fishing, traveling, moving goods, exploring more easily*
Why are rivers important today?	*for jobs in factories and power plants, for shipping goods*
How will you decide where to live when you are grown up?	*Answers will vary but may relate to being near a job, family, or a recreational opportunity; avoiding natural disasters; enjoying the beauty of a place; or returning to a previous home.*
How was the topic "a place to call home" shown in "Why Live Near a River?"	*It explained why many people live near rivers, especially back when pioneers were figuring out a good place to settle. It also told some bad things about rivers that people should think about now.*
How was the topic "a place to call home" shown in "New Land, New Life"?	*The story was about a community looking for a new place to call home because they needed to move somewhere else to be safer.*
Why do you think these selections were paired together?	*They both talk about things to think about when deciding where to live, especially having water nearby, but they give different problems to think about. Also, one gives information you can use today, and the other one tells about a certain problem long ago.*

Plan Your Writing

Graphic Organizer

Think about how living near a river can be both good and bad. You will be asked to compare the advantages and disadvantages of places where people decide to live. Use the charts below to organize your writing.

Why Live Near a River?	
Advantages:	**Disadvantages:**

New Land, New Life	
Advantages:	**Disadvantages:**

Write an Essay

Write an essay to compare the advantages and disadvantages of places where people decide to live. Give your essay a title. Include details from the selections. Use transitions to connect your ideas.

Title: _____

_____

_____

_____

_____

_____

_____

_____

_____

_____

_____

_____

_____

Meeting the Father of a Country

Student Objective: Students will understand that individuals, events, and ideas shape a country's leaders and its history.

Essential Question:

What was the first United States president like?

Topic Introduction: Share the unit title and essential question with students. Explain to students that the United States was the first country to be led by a president. Many countries now have presidents. Tell students that they will read two selections about the first United States president.

Paired Text Selections:

Assessment Materials:

Lesson Plan

1. Introduce the Selection

Tell students they will read a selection about a leader of the United States whose actions made life better for others.

2. Read Aloud the Selection

Reproduce the selection and distribute it to each student. Students will use this for all activities within the unit. Point out that some of the words in the text are defined at the bottom of the pages.

Have students follow along silently as you read aloud. Direct students' attention to graphic elements or visual aids.

3. Introduce Vocabulary

Reproduce the Dictionary and the Apply Vocabulary activities and distribute them to each student.

Dictionary: Read aloud the vocabulary words and definitions. Discuss definitions and usage as needed.

Have students find each vocabulary word in the selection and read the context sentence. Then have students complete <u>one</u> of the leveled activities below:

- Basic level: Write the context sentence on the lines below its definition.

- Challenge level: Write a new sentence using the vocabulary word and share the sentence with a partner, a small group, or the whole class.

Apply Vocabulary: Have students complete the activity independently, with a partner, or in small groups.

4. Students Read the Selection

Have students read the selection independently, with a partner, or in small groups.

5. Analyze the Selection: Oral Close Reading Activity

Have students number each paragraph in the selection before they begin the close reading discussion.

Use the script on the following page to guide students in discussing the selection. Explain that close reading will help them notice important parts of the selection. Encourage students to refer to the selection as necessary to find the information they need.

To support visual learners, you may wish to cover up the sample responses and reproduce and distribute the discussion questions for students to refer to.

6. Understand the Selection

Reproduce the Answer Questions activity and distribute it to each student. Have students complete the activity independently. Encourage students to refer to the selection as necessary to help them answer the questions and/or to check their answers.

You may wish to use this as a formative assessment to determine students' understanding of the text.

7. Write About the Selection

Reproduce the Write About It activity and distribute it to each student.

Graphic Organizer: Have students complete the graphic organizer in small groups.

Writing Prompt: Have students complete the writing assignment independently on a separate sheet of paper.

Oral Close Reading Activity

Ask students the following text-dependent questions and have them refer to the selection as needed.

Questions	Sample Responses
In the first paragraph, what does the word "colonists" probably mean?	*people who live in a colony*
How did you figure it out?	*It looks like "colony" with the suffix "ist," which means a person.*
What details from the selection show that George Washington liked dogs?	*He had several dogs. He took his dog Sweet Lips with him when he went to Philadelphia. He also took care of General Howe's dog and returned it to its owner.*
In the second paragraph, what do the words "rode out" probably mean?	*went hunting*
How did you figure it out?	*He liked to hunt, and hounds are good at hunting, so that's probably what he did with his hounds.*
Who lost a dog during a battle?	*General Howe*
Who found the dog?	*Washington's men*
In the fourth paragraph, what does the word "pooch" probably mean?	*dog*
How did you figure it out?	*They're talking about the lost dog they found. It makes sense to feed and brush a dog.*
Look at the pronouns in the second sentence of the message to Howe. Whom does the pronoun "He" refer to?	*George Washington*
Whom does the pronoun "him" refer to?	*General Howe*
What does "fell into his hands" probably mean?	*He got ahold of it, he ended up with it.*
Why was it clever for Washington to return General Howe's dog?	*He used the lost dog as an excuse to send someone who could look around Howe's headquarters.*
Is this text fiction or nonfiction?	*nonfiction*
Why?	*because it tells facts about George Washington and about history*

The Generals and Their Dogs

Most people know that George Washington was the first president of the United States. Washington was born before the United States was a country. At that time, people lived in colonies ruled by the British. The colonists decided they wanted to make their own rules. Washington and other leaders met in Philadelphia. They talked about forming an independent country.

Most people don't know much about Washington's character. For instance, Washington was a huge dog lover! Fox hunting was one of his favorite pastimes. Washington rode out with his hounds at least once a week. His favorite hound was named Sweet Lips. Washington took her with him whenever he went to Philadelphia.

The colonists decided to fight the British for their freedom. The war was called the Revolutionary War. Washington was commander in chief of the colonial army. In one of the battles, the colonists attacked the British at dawn. They surprised the sleepy British troops and their commander, General Howe. However, Washington's attack plan had several mistakes. The British still won the battle. But General Howe lost his dog.

Washington's men found the lost dog on the battlefield. It was wearing a collar with the owner's name on it. Washington took the pooch to his tent, fed it, and

forming: making, starting

troops: soldiers

brushed it. Washington's aide sent a polite message to the British commander:

> General Washington's compliments to General Howe. He does himself the pleasure to return him a Dog, which accidentally fell into his hands, and by the inscription on the Collar, appears to belong to General Howe.

History has lost the reply from General Howe. However, we know the dog was returned. Everyone stopped fighting long enough to take the dog back to General Howe. General Washington's messenger went to General Howe's headquarters with the dog.

Washington was not just a dog lover. He was also a clever general. He never missed a chance to get information about the enemy. Could the messenger with the dog have seen something? Did he bring back information to General Washington? We can only wonder.

compliments: greetings

inscription: short written label

Dictionary

Write a sentence using each vocabulary word.

colony: an area that belongs to a country far away

_____

_____

independent: free from the control of others

_____

_____

character: the way a person thinks, feels, and acts; what a person is like

_____

_____

pastime: a hobby; a fun way of spending time

_____

_____

hound: a type of dog used for hunting that has a very good sense of smell

_____

_____

pleasure: good feeling, joy

_____

_____

headquarters: a place where leaders organize a group

_____

_____

Reading Paired Text • EMC 1373 • © Evan-Moor Corp.

Apply Vocabulary

Complete each sentence using a word from the word box.

Word Box

character	colony	headquarters	hound
independent	pastime	pleasure	

1. It was a _____ to meet another student who can speak Greek like I can.

2. The _____ barked at the strange noise.

3. Ms. Soto addressed her letter to the company's _____.

4. My teacher's favorite _____ is singing.

5. He says he cares about nature, but he showed his true

   _____ when he threw a candy wrapper on the ground.

6. She tried out for our town's _____ baseball team, not her school's team.

7. The members of the _____ worked together.

Write one new sentence. Use a word from the word box.

1. _____

   _____

Answer Questions

Read and answer each question.

1. What was George Washington's role in the Revolutionary War?

    Ⓐ British soldier

    Ⓑ British spy

    Ⓒ president of the United States

    Ⓓ commander in chief of the colonists

2. What is true about both Washington and Howe?

    Ⓐ They both wanted the colonists to be independent.

    Ⓑ They were both dog lovers.

    Ⓒ They both wrote polite notes.

    Ⓓ They both liked to attack at dawn.

3. Where did General Howe lose his dog?

    Ⓐ in Philadelphia

    Ⓑ at British headquarters

    Ⓒ on the battlefield

    Ⓓ on a fox hunting ride

4. Why did Washington want to send a messenger with General Howe's dog?

    Ⓐ to get information about the British army

    Ⓑ to see how the British treated their dogs

    Ⓒ to make everyone stop fighting

    Ⓓ to trade the dog for information

5. How did Washington know who owned the lost dog?

    _____

    _____

6. Explain why the colonists fought in the Revolutionary War.

    _____

    _____

    _____

Write About It

Graphic Organizer

Think about General Washington and General Howe. What did they
have in common? How were they different? You will be asked to write
a compare-and-contrast essay about the two generals. Use the chart below
to organize your writing.

	General Washington	General Howe
Which side he led		
How he commanded		
How he treated his dogs		

Writing Prompt

On a separate sheet of paper, write two paragraphs to compare General
Washington and General Howe. Use details from the selection in your
response.

Lesson Plan

1. Introduce the Selection

Tell students they will read a selection about a real-life folk hero whose actions as a child influenced the leader he became. Tell students that the original selection was written over 200 years ago and that some of the words and sentences will sound old-fashioned.

2. Read Aloud the Selection

Reproduce the selection and distribute it to each student. Students will use this for all activities within the unit.

Have students follow along silently as you read aloud. Direct students' attention to graphic elements or visual aids.

3. Introduce Vocabulary

Reproduce the Dictionary and the Apply Vocabulary activities and distribute them to each student.

Dictionary: Read aloud the vocabulary words and definitions. Discuss definitions and usage as needed.

Have students find each vocabulary word in the selection and read the context sentence. Then have students complete <u>one</u> of the leveled activities below:

- Basic level: Write the context sentence on the lines below its definition.

- Challenge level: Write a new sentence using the vocabulary word and share the sentence with a partner, a small group, or the whole class.

Apply Vocabulary: Have students complete the activity independently, with a partner, or in small groups.

4. Students Read the Selection

Have students read the selection independently, with a partner, or in small groups.

5. Analyze the Selection: Oral Close Reading Activity

Have students number each paragraph in the selection before they begin the close reading discussion.

Use the script on the following page to guide students in discussing the selection. Explain that close reading will help them notice important parts of the selection. Encourage students to refer to the selection as necessary to find the information they need.

To support visual learners, you may wish to cover up the sample responses and reproduce and distribute the discussion questions for students to refer to.

6. Understand the Selection

Reproduce the Answer Questions activity and distribute it to each student. Have students complete the activity independently. Encourage students to refer to the selection as necessary to help them answer the questions and/or to check their answers.

You may wish to use this as a formative assessment to determine students' understanding of the text.

7. Write About the Selection

Reproduce the Write About It activity and distribute it to each student.

Graphic Organizer: Have students complete the graphic organizer in small groups.

Writing Prompt: Have students complete the writing assignment independently on a separate sheet of paper.

Oral Close Reading Activity

Ask students the following text-dependent questions and have them refer to the selection as needed.

Questions	Sample Responses
Is this story about a real person or a fictional person?	*real*
Is this story fiction or nonfiction?	*fiction*
Which sentence tells you that?	*"It was most likely made up."*
What did George do with the hatchet?	*He hacked at pea sticks and chopped bark off a cherry tree.*
What did George's father think was very important in a young person?	*honesty, telling the truth*
What did George's father say he would do to see an honest boy?	*ride 50 miles*
Give another sentence from the selection that shows how much the truth is worth to George's father.	*"Telling me the truth is worth more to me than any tree."* or *"It is worth more than a thousand trees with fruits of gold."*
Why does George's father think young people lie?	*They make mistakes. They are afraid of being punished.*
What will George's father do if George tells him about a mistake?	*honor and love him more*
What mistake does George make?	*He kills his father's cherry tree.*
What does his father do when George admits he killed the tree?	*He stretches out his arms to his son.*
In the fifth paragraph of the story, what does the word "hotly" mean?	*loudly, angrily*
How did you figure it out?	*He would probably be upset and yell when he saw his tree cut. Later on, it says he lost his anger, so he must have been angry. The picture shows his father looking angry.*
What did George learn from his experience of chopping down the cherry tree?	*People will respect you for telling the truth even if you have made a mistake.*
How did the illustrations help you understand the story?	*They show how big the tree was, how he cut off the bark, how angry his father was when he asked George about it.*

The Legend of the Cherry Tree

adapted from *The Life of George Washington* by M.L. Weems (1809)

"The Legend of the Cherry Tree" is a very old story about George Washington. It was most likely made up. However, it is a legend still shared with children today.

Mr. Washington wished to teach his little son George the value of truth. "I would ride 50 miles to see the little boy whose heart is honest," he began. "We may trust every word he says. But, how different is the boy who does not tell the truth. Nobody can believe a word he says!" He paused and looked at George squarely in the eyes. "George, you are but a little boy yet. You do not have experience or knowledge. You may often make mistakes. Whenever you might do anything wrong, never tell a lie to hide it. Be brave and tell me of it. I will not punish you. Instead, I promise that I will honor and love you the more for it."

Later, when George was about six years old, he was made the owner of a hatchet! "A hatchet is not a toy," his father warned. "You must always use it with caution. A hatchet can do much harm if used carelessly."

George looked at the shiny, sharp blade. "I promise, Pa. I'll use it well."

George was very fond of his hatchet. He was forever going about chopping everything in his way. One day he was in the garden, where he liked to hack at his mother's pea sticks. George tried his hatchet on the trunk of a beautiful young cherry tree. He chopped the bark terribly. George slept poorly that evening.

The next morning, George's father saw what had happened to his favorite tree. He came into the house and hotly asked who had done it. Nobody knew anything about it. Before long, George and his hatchet appeared. "George," said his father, "do you know who killed my beautiful little cherry tree?"

This was a tough question, and George faltered for a moment. Then, looking at his father, he bravely cried out, "I cannot tell a lie, Pa. You know I cannot tell a lie. I cut it with my hatchet."

George's father lost his anger. He stretched out his arms to his son. "You have spoken with honor. Telling me the truth is worth more to me than any tree. It is worth more than a thousand trees with fruits of gold," he said.

Dictionary

Write a sentence using each vocabulary word.

value: how important something is

_____

_____

squarely: directly, straight

_____

_____

hatchet: a small ax with a short handle

_____

_____

caution: care taken to avoid danger or mistakes

_____

_____

hack: to cut roughly

_____

_____

falter: to speak in an unsteady voice

_____

_____

Apply Vocabulary

Complete each sentence using a word from the word box.

Word Box

caution	faltered	hacked
hatchet	squarely	value

1. Jill used a _____ to split the coconut open.

2. Hit the ball _____ in the middle to make it go far.

3. Workers _____ the weeds down to prevent a wildfire.

4. Sonya saw the _____ of practice after she won the race.

5. "I don't know the answer," Ravi _____.

6. Roberto rode down the slippery streets with _____.

Write two new sentences. Use a word from the word box in each.

1. _____

_____

2. _____

_____

Answer Questions

Read and answer each question.

1. What did Mr. Washington teach his son George to do?

   Ⓐ pick cherries

   Ⓑ tell the truth

   Ⓒ plant a cherry tree

   Ⓓ avoid making mistakes

2. Which sentence from the selection is a warning from George's father?

   Ⓐ "Nobody can believe a word he says!"

   Ⓑ "You may often make mistakes."

   Ⓒ "Telling me the truth is worth more to me than any tree."

   Ⓓ "A hatchet can do much harm if used carelessly."

3. Why did George chop the cherry tree?

   Ⓐ to practice cutting different kinds of plants

   Ⓑ to get some peas and cherries

   Ⓒ to test his father's promise

   Ⓓ to show his father he was angry

4. Why did George falter when his father asked who killed the tree?

   Ⓐ He did not know who did it.

   Ⓑ He was waiting for his father to calm down.

   Ⓒ He was thinking of lying but changed his mind.

   Ⓓ He was surprised anyone had noticed it.

5. What does this legend help explain about George Washington after he grew up?

   _____

   _____

   _____

6. Describe George's father's character. Use details from the selection.

   _____

   _____

   _____

Write About It

Think about the promises that George and his father made to each other. You will be asked to write about each person and his promise. Use the chart below to organize your writing.

	George	George's father
The promise he made		
How he lived up to or didn't live up to the promise		
How the promise affected him		

On a separate sheet of paper, write two paragraphs to compare the promises George and his father made and what the promises say about each person. Use details from the selection in your response.

Meeting the Father of a Country

Topic: Meeting the Father of a Country

Essential Question: What was the first United States president like?

Tying It Together

Use the script below to guide students in discussing the essential question and what they have learned about the topic from the paired selections. Feel free to expand on these questions and responses.

To support visual learners, you may wish to cover up the sample responses and reproduce and distribute the discussion questions for students to refer to.

Questions	Sample Responses
What would George Washington's father probably have thought about George returning the dog?	*He would have thought it was right to return something that was lost. George behaved honorably.*
What was the first United States president like as a child?	*He liked to play in the garden and cut things down. He felt guilty when he killed the tree. He kept his promise to tell the truth and was honest with his father.*
What was he like when he grew up?	*He loved dogs and fox hunting. He worked to make the U.S. a country. He was a clever general but still made mistakes. He was honorable and didn't steal.*
How did Washington treat people?	*He treated them honestly and politely. He respected them.*
How did we see this in the selections?	*He didn't lie to his father, even though he was afraid of getting in trouble. He wrote a very polite note to General Howe. He gave respect to General Howe as a dog lover even though he was fighting him in a war.*
How was the topic "meeting the father of a country" shown in "The Generals and Their Dogs"?	*It describes Washington during the time the U.S. was being formed, right before he became president.*
How was the topic "meeting the father of a country" shown in "The Legend of the Cherry Tree"?	*It describes Washington when he was very young. It shows him learning a lesson that stayed with him when he became president.*
Why do you think these selections were paired together?	*They both describe Washington's character, but at different times of his life. They are both stories, but one is probably made up. They both show his honesty and mention things he liked to do, like fox hunting and chopping plants in the garden.*

Plan Your Writing

Think about what you learned from the two selections about George Washington at different times of his life. You will be asked to describe his character as a young boy and as a general and compare how he changed and stayed the same. Use the chart below to organize your writing.

Character description	
As a young boy:	**How he changed:**
As a general:	**How he stayed the same:**

Write an Essay

Write an essay to compare George Washington's character as a young boy and as a general and describe how he changed and stayed the same. Give your essay a title. Include details from the selections. Use transitions to connect your ideas.

Title: _____

_____

_____

_____

_____

_____

_____

_____

_____

_____

_____

_____

_____

Picturing the World

Student Objective: Students will understand that maps are drawings of places on Earth and that it took a lot of time and effort to figure out where all the lands and oceans are.

Essential Question:

How did we figure out what our world looks like?

Topic Introduction: Share the unit title and essential question with students. Then explain that ships and boats were once the only way to get around. Few people traveled and knew about other places. Tell students that they will read two selections about how curiosity led to a better understanding of the world.

Paired Text Selections:

Assessment Materials:

Lesson Plan

1. **Introduce the Selection**

   Tell students they will read about the first maps that people made. Display a world map in the classroom. Explain to students that maps show our surroundings, near and far.

2. **Read Aloud the Selection**

   Reproduce the selection and distribute it to each student. Students will use this for all activities within the unit. Point out that some of the words in the text are defined at the bottom of the pages.

   Have students follow along silently as you read aloud. Direct students' attention to graphic elements or visual aids.

3. **Introduce Vocabulary**

   Reproduce the Dictionary and the Apply Vocabulary activities and distribute them to each student.

   Dictionary: Read aloud the vocabulary words and definitions. Point out that *trade* is a multiple-meaning word, or a homonym. Discuss definitions and usage as needed.

   Have students find each vocabulary word in the selection and read the context sentence. Then have students complete <u>one</u> of the leveled activities below:

   - Basic level: Write the context sentence on the lines below its definition.

   - Challenge level: Write a new sentence using the vocabulary word and share the sentence with a partner, a small group, or the whole class.

   Apply Vocabulary: Have students complete the activity independently, with a partner, or in small groups.

4. **Students Read the Selection**

   Have students read the selection independently, with a partner, or in small groups.

5. **Analyze the Selection:**
   Oral Close Reading Activity

   Have students number each paragraph in the selection before they begin the close reading discussion.

   Use the script on the following page to guide students in discussing the selection. Explain that close reading will help them notice important parts of the selection. Encourage students to refer to the selection as necessary to find the information they need.

   To support visual learners, you may wish to cover up the sample responses and reproduce and distribute the discussion questions for students to refer to.

6. **Understand the Selection**

   Reproduce the Answer Questions activity and distribute it to each student. Have students complete the activity independently. Encourage students to refer to the selection as necessary to help them answer the questions and/or to check their answers.

   You may wish to use this as a formative assessment to determine students' understanding of the text.

7. **Write About the Selection**

   Reproduce the Write About It activity and distribute it to each student.

   Graphic Organizer: Have students complete the graphic organizer in small groups.

   Writing Prompt: Have students complete the writing assignment independently on a separate sheet of paper.

Oral Close Reading Activity

Ask students the following text-dependent questions and have them refer to the selection as needed.

Questions	Sample Responses
What does the author compare a puzzle picture to?	*a map*
What do the pieces of the puzzle represent in exploration?	*lands that explorers find*
What three areas did Claudius Ptolemy's book describe?	*Europe, Asia, Africa*
Why did he include only these areas?	*He didn't know there were any other areas.*
From where did he get information about these areas?	*from earlier geographers, news records, and merchants' travel diaries*
In the third paragraph, what does the phrase "places beyond those in Ptolemy's book" refer to?	*lands that did not appear in his book, places Europeans had never seen*
What did Columbus set out to do?	*to find a new trade route to India*
What did he find instead?	*islands near North America/the New World*
Columbus called the people he met in the New World "Indians." Why did he most likely use that word?	*He thought he was in India.*
Where did the two mapmakers get information for the map they published in 1507?	*from Ptolemy's book and the notes and drawings from Christopher Columbus's and Amerigo Vespucci's travels*
What is special about their map?	*It was the first map that named America.*
How do the two maps in the selection look different?	*The 1507 map shows North America much smaller than the modern map does.*
How do you explain that?	*The 1507 map shows that people had not explored all of the American continents yet. They knew only part of what was there.*

Putting the Pieces Together

Have you ever assembled the pieces of a jigsaw puzzle? It can be a challenge to make the picture on the puzzle box. Now imagine completing the puzzle without having a picture! That is what early explorers did before there were maps, or pictures of the world. As they traveled to new places, they added pieces to the growing picture.

Claudius Ptolemy [TALL-uh-me] was a mathematician and geographer. He wrote the first geography book around the year 150. He used information from earlier geographers, news records, and the travel diaries of merchants. Ptolemy's book gave information about Europe, Asia, and Africa. Other people used the information from this book to draw the first map of the world.

In the 1400s, explorers from Europe set out across the Atlantic Ocean to places beyond those in Ptolemy's book. The ships' recorders made careful descriptions and drawings of the lands they found.

Explorer Christopher Columbus was familiar with Ptolemy's ancient book. Columbus set sail from Spain in 1492 to find a new trade route to India. But he believed the world was smaller. This mistake led him to islands near what is now North America.

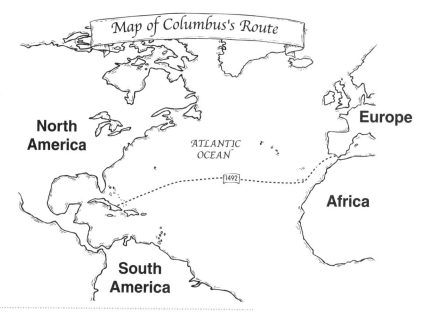

Map of Columbus's Route

North America

ATLANTIC OCEAN

1492

Europe

Africa

South America

geographer: someone who studies where land and water are

ancient: very old

He called the people on these islands "Indians." A short time later, Amerigo Vespucci crossed the Atlantic. But he aimed farther south. He sailed the entire north and east coasts of a huge new land. Then he realized he had found a New World that was not on any map. It was later named South America. Columbus and Vespucci took careful notes of what they saw and made drawings of the coast.

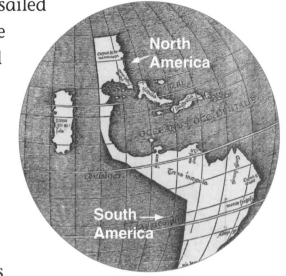

from the 1507 world map

In 1507, two mapmakers created a map using information from Ptolemy, Columbus, and Vespucci. The mapmakers named the New World "America" in honor of explorer Amerigo Vespucci. However, they still didn't know how wide North and South America were. It took more explorers and many more years to fill out the map.

Today, we consult maps that show all the lands on Earth. Some show boundaries between states or countries. Some show land features, such as mountains and lakes. Some show the weather in different areas. We no longer have to find land to make maps. Now we use maps to find our way on land!

from a modern world map

Dictionary

Write a sentence using each vocabulary word.

assemble: to put together

_____

_____

merchant: someone who sells things

_____

_____

trade: buying and selling goods

_____

_____

consult: to look at; to get information from

_____

_____

boundary: a line that marks the edge of an area

_____

_____

feature: a part or detail that stands out

_____

_____

Apply Vocabulary

Complete each sentence using a word from the word box.

Word Box		
assemble	boundaries	consult
features	merchants	trade

1. A fence and a driveway mark the _____ of their yard.

2. The farmer's market is a busy _____ center in our town.

3. Local _____ donated some products for our school fundraiser.

4. Marco wants to _____ a plumber about the leaky faucet.

5. Mrs. Brown will _____ the winning poems into a class book.

6. The campground has modern _____ such as showers and electricity.

Write two new sentences. Use a word from the word box in each.

1. _____

   _____

2. _____

   _____

Answer Questions

Read and answer each question.

1. How did explorers in the 1400s help people picture the world?

   Ⓐ They found lands that were unknown.

   Ⓑ They collected jigsaw puzzles.

   Ⓒ They improved shipbuilding.

   Ⓓ They traded with people in Europe.

2. Who was Claudius Ptolemy?

   Ⓐ an explorer

   Ⓑ a merchant

   Ⓒ a geographer

   Ⓓ a ship's recorder

3. Why did Columbus end up finding islands near the New World?

   Ⓐ He made drawings of what he saw.

   Ⓑ He could not find the Atlantic Ocean.

   Ⓒ His ships could not go all the way to India.

   Ⓓ The world was bigger than he thought.

4. How do we use maps today?

   Ⓐ to explore unknown places

   Ⓑ to find new trade routes

   Ⓒ to get information

   Ⓓ to put puzzles together

5. Why was America named in honor of Amerigo Vespucci?

_____

_____

_____

6. Compare the two maps in the selection. Did the shape of the land change, or just the maps? Give evidence from the selection.

_____

_____

_____

Write About It

Graphic Organizer

Think about how the world map has changed from ancient times to today.
You will be asked to compare the differences. Use the chart below to
organize your writing.

	Ancient map	Modern map
Differences in land		
Differences in oceans		

Writing Prompt

On a separate sheet of paper, write a two-paragraph letter to Amerigo
Vespucci to compare the modern world map with the map from ancient
times. Use details from the selection in your letter.

Lesson Plan

1. Introduce the Selection

Tell students they will read a play about how being curious led some children to make close observations.

2. Read Aloud the Selection

Reproduce the selection and distribute it to each student. Students will use this for all activities within the unit. Point out that some of the words in the text are defined at the bottom of the pages.

Have students follow along silently as you read aloud. Direct students' attention to graphic elements or visual aids.

3. Introduce Vocabulary

Reproduce the Dictionary and the Apply Vocabulary activities and distribute them to each student.

Dictionary: Read aloud the vocabulary words and definitions. Discuss definitions and usage as needed.

Have students find each vocabulary word in the selection and read the context sentence. Then have students complete <u>one</u> of the leveled activities below:

- Basic level: Write the context sentence on the lines below its definition.

- Challenge level: Write a new sentence using the vocabulary word and share the sentence with a partner, a small group, or the whole class.

Apply Vocabulary: Have students complete the activity independently, with a partner, or in small groups.

4. Students Read the Selection

Have students read the selection independently, with a partner, or in small groups.

5. Analyze the Selection: Oral Close Reading Activity

Have students number each paragraph of dialogue in the play before they begin the close reading discussion.

Use the script on the following page to guide students in discussing the selection. Explain that close reading will help them notice important parts of the selection. Encourage students to refer to the selection as necessary to find the information they need.

To support visual learners, you may wish to cover up the sample responses and reproduce and distribute the discussion questions for students to refer to.

6. Understand the Selection

Reproduce the Answer Questions activity and distribute it to each student. Have students complete the activity independently. Encourage students to refer to the selection as necessary to help them answer the questions and/or to check their answers.

You may wish to use this as a formative assessment to determine students' understanding of the text.

7. Write About the Selection

Reproduce the Write About It activity and distribute it to each student.

Graphic Organizer: Have students complete the graphic organizer in small groups.

Writing Prompt: Have students complete the writing assignment independently on a separate sheet of paper.

Oral Close Reading Activity

Ask students the following text-dependent questions and have them refer to the selection as needed.

Questions	Sample Responses
What is the setting of the play?	*Greece, by the sea, a long time ago*
How can you tell?	*In the illustration, the characters are dressed in clothes from long ago, and it shows the sea. Kara mentions Greece.*
Which child seems to be the oldest?	*Alexander*
How can you tell?	*He seems to know the most; he explains things to the others.*
Give an example from the selection that shows that Alexander is probably the oldest.	*"I think you're mistaken about the world being flat with edges." "There is one bright light they can use that won't fall—the North Star." "Your eyes are fooling you into thinking that the world is flat. Watch Father's ship and tell me what you see."*
What are the children wondering about the world?	*what its shape is, whether it has an edge or an end*
Why does Alexander point out that there are hills and mountains around them?	*to show that the world is probably not flat*
What similes does Kara use?	*"like a flat pan of water," "as soft as cotton," "as black as a thundercloud"*
What do these phrases help you understand?	*The sea looks like it is flat and has edges; the sky looks soft to Kara, and she likes the clouds; the sea is extremely dark.*
What helps the sailors see where they are going at night?	*the North Star*
Why is this better than candles?	*The candles won't make very much light; they could fall over.*
Who comes over the hill singing?	*Mother*
How can you tell who it is?	*Mother enters the dialogue after someone comes over the hill; Kara talks about her appearing and calls her "Mother."*
The children see less of Father's ship as it sails away and more of their mother as she comes over the hill. What does that show the children about the world?	*The world might be round or curved like a hill.*

The Edge of the World

Hector, Kara, and Alexander wave to their father, who is a merchant. He is sailing to another city to sell his goods.

Kara: I think the sea looks like a flat pan of water. What if a storm makes it spill over? Where will Father's ship go?

Alexander: I don't know how big the world is, but I've never heard a sailor claim to run out of sea.

Hector: Well, what if Father's ship falls over the edge of the water? The men will turn back before they get too close, won't they?

Alexander: I think you're mistaken about the world being flat with edges, Hector. Look at the hill behind us and the mountains just south of us.

Kara: I want Father to take me with him on his next journey. When we get to the horizon, I will stretch my fingers and tickle the sky. I expect it to feel as soft as cotton.

Alexander *(laughing)*: I've seen men climb to the tops of mountains, but none has boasted about touching the sky.

Kara: Father said he would be gone from Greece for several days. How will the crew navigate the ship at night?

Hector: They should use giant candles to see in the dark.

Kara: The sea at night is as black as a thundercloud, so candles will not do much good.

Hector: I suppose the candles could fall and start a fire if the ship isn't steady. Then what would the men do?

Alexander: There is one bright light they can use that won't fall—the North Star. The captain uses it to know where north is and the other directions, too.

Hector: If I were the captain, I would stay close to the shore so I wouldn't go off the end.

Alexander: Your eyes are fooling you into thinking the world is flat. Watch Father's ship and tell me what you see.

Alexander points to Father's ship as it nears the horizon.

Hector: Part of the ship's hull seems to be under water!

Kara: And now I see only the sails of the ship.

Hector: Hey! Now I see only the tops of the sails! What's happening?

There is a voice singing behind the hill. The children turn to see a woman coming into view. First they see just her head scarf, then her shawl. When she reaches the hilltop, they see all of her.

Mother: Has your father's ship sailed?

Kara: Something about the way you appeared, Mother, reminds me of how Father's ship gradually disappeared.

Alexander: So the world might be rounded, like a hill.

Hector: And Father's ship won't fall off!

----

hull: the main part of a boat, including the bottom and sides

shawl: a long piece of cloth worn over the shoulders

Dictionary

Write a sentence using each vocabulary word.

claim: to say you did or can do something hard or unusual

_____

_____

mistaken: wrong; not correct

_____

_____

horizon: the line where the earth and the sky seem to meet

_____

_____

boast: to brag; to talk with too much pride

_____

_____

navigate: to plan where to go and stay on course

_____

_____

gradually: slowly; little by little

_____

_____

Apply Vocabulary

Complete each sentence using a word from the word box.

Word Box

boast	claim	gradually
horizon	mistaken	navigate

1. Dad was _____ about what time the bike ride started, and he arrived too early.

2. Laura saw distant storm clouds on the _____.

3. I _____ learned the song after I heard it many times.

4. The new student used a map to _____ around the school.

5. Jerry likes to _____ about his science fair award.

6. Our cousins _____ to be able to run faster than a horse.

Write two new sentences. Use a word from the word box in each.

1. _____

_____

2. _____

_____

Name: _____

Answer Questions

Read and answer each question.

1. If Kara drew the world, it would probably look like a _____.

    Ⓐ can

    Ⓑ hill

    Ⓒ tray

    Ⓓ bowl

2. Which sentence describes the way the ship nears the horizon?

    Ⓐ The entire ship looks like it is falling off the edge.

    Ⓑ The ship seems to be sinking in the water.

    Ⓒ The sky seems to swallow the ship from top to bottom.

    Ⓓ The ship looks like it is touching the sky.

3. Hector is afraid that _____.

    Ⓐ the sea will run out of water

    Ⓑ Father's ship will sail off the edge

    Ⓒ Father will be away too long

    Ⓓ the ship is staying close to shore

4. How does Alexander help the younger children think about the world's shape?

    Ⓐ He answers all of the children's questions.

    Ⓑ He talks about men who climbed mountains.

    Ⓒ He explains why the North Star is important.

    Ⓓ He calls their attention to things to observe.

5. Explain how the captain of Father's ship navigates at night and why.

    _____

    _____

    _____

6. How does Mother's arrival help the children think about the shape of the world?

    _____

    _____

    _____

Write About It

Graphic Organizer

Imagine that Kara gets to travel with her father on his next journey and that she keeps a travel diary of her observations. You will be asked to write several diary entries based on the observations made in the play. Use the chart below to organize your writing.

As she sails farther from shore:

While at sea:

At night:

When she sees land:

Writing Prompt

On a separate sheet of paper, write four diary entries that Kara could write to inform others about her journey with her father. Kara's observations should be based on details from the play.

Picturing the World

Topic: Picturing the World
Essential Question: How did we figure out what our world looks like?

Tying It Together

Use the script below to guide students in discussing the essential question and what they have learned about the topic from the paired selections. Feel free to expand on these questions and responses.

To support visual learners, you may wish to cover up the sample responses and reproduce and distribute the discussion questions for students to refer to.

Questions	Sample Responses
What did most people think about the world in ancient times?	*They knew only about the area where they lived. They didn't know about other lands. They thought there were only three continents. They wondered if the world had an edge or boundary.*
What kinds of people helped our knowledge of the world grow?	*geographers, explorers, ships' recorders, merchants, anyone who traveled*
What qualities did all of these people have?	*They were good observers; adventurous; paid attention to details.*
How did these people help us figure out what our world looks like?	*They took notes about where they went; wrote descriptions of what they saw; drew pictures of new lands; kept diaries. Ptolemy wrote a book using all the information he could gather. Mapmakers made maps based on everyone's notes and drawings.*
How was the topic "picturing the world" shown in "Putting the Pieces Together"?	*It described how explorers went out looking for new lands. They were trying to figure out where everything was and easier ways to get there.*
How was the topic "picturing the world" shown in "The Edge of the World"?	*It had kids wondering about the shape of the world, where their father's ship was going, if he would have problems at night or fall off the edge of the world.*
Why do you think these selections were paired together?	*They both talk about learning where other places are, but one gives facts from history and the other tells a story about what it was like living in the time when we didn't know about the whole world.*

Plan Your Writing

Graphic Organizer

Thing about how the explorers and the children in the play used their eyes like tools to picture the world. You will be asked to explain what they saw and their conclusions. Use the chart below to organize your writing.

	What they saw	Their conclusions
Christopher Columbus		
Amerigo Vespucci		
Children in the play		

Write an Essay

Writing Prompt

Write an essay to explain how the explorers and the children in the play used what they saw and drew conclusions to picture their world. Give your essay a title. Include details from the selections. Use transitions to connect your ideas.

Title: _____

_____

_____

_____

_____

_____

_____

_____

_____

_____

_____

_____

_____

_____

Changing with Our Surroundings

Student Objective:
Students will understand that every living thing must be able to change as its surroundings change, and that without that ability, it will not survive.

Essential Question:
How do living things respond when the environment changes?

Topic Introduction:
Share the unit title and essential question with students. Explain to students that every living thing has basic needs. Tell students they will read two selections about how living things respond to their environments.

Paired Text Selections:

Assessment Materials:

Lesson Plan

1. Introduce the Selection

Tell students they will read about meat-eating plants. Review with students that all green plants make their own food using energy from the sun and that most plants get nutrients from the soil.

2. Read Aloud the Selection

Reproduce the selection and distribute it to each student. Students will use this for all activities within the unit. Point out that some of the words in the text are defined at the bottom of the pages.

Have students follow along silently as you read aloud. Direct students' attention to graphic elements or visual aids.

3. Introduce Vocabulary

Reproduce the Dictionary and the Apply Vocabulary activities and distribute them to each student.

Dictionary: Read aloud the vocabulary words and definitions. Discuss definitions and usage as needed.

Have students find each vocabulary word in the selection and read the context sentence. Then have students complete <u>one</u> of the leveled activities below:

- Basic level: Write the context sentence on the lines below its definition.

- Challenge level: Write a new sentence using the vocabulary word and share the sentence with a partner, a small group, or the whole class.

Apply Vocabulary: Have students complete the activity independently, with a partner, or in small groups.

4. Students Read the Selection

Have students read the selection independently, with a partner, or in small groups.

5. Analyze the Selection: Oral Close Reading Activity

Have students number each paragraph in the selection before they begin the close reading discussion.

Use the script on the following page to guide students in discussing the selection. Explain that close reading will help them notice important parts of the selection. Encourage students to refer to the selection as necessary to find the information they need.

To support visual learners, you may wish to cover up the sample responses and reproduce and distribute the discussion questions for students to refer to.

6. Understand the Selection

Reproduce the Answer Questions activity and distribute it to each student. Have students complete the activity independently. Encourage students to refer to the selection as necessary to help them answer the questions and/or to check their answers.

You may wish to use this as a formative assessment to determine students' understanding of the text.

7. Write About the Selection

Reproduce the Write About It activity and distribute it to each student.

Graphic Organizer: Have students complete the graphic organizer in small groups.

Writing Prompt: Have students complete the writing assignment independently on a separate sheet of paper.

Oral Close Reading Activity

Ask students the following text-dependent questions and have them refer to the selection as needed.

Questions	Sample Responses
How are meat-eating plants similar to other plants?	*They make their own food.*
How are they different?	*They eat bugs and small animals, too.*
The author calls the Venus' flytrap a "deadly plant." Why?	*It kills bugs.*
How do the plants attract their meal?	*They make a sweet liquid.*
Why don't the bugs leave after they drink the liquid on the plant?	*They are trapped.*
What part of a Venus' flytrap makes the leaves shut?	*the hairs on its leaves*
What part of a Venus' flytrap keeps the bug from escaping?	*the teeth*
In the sixth paragraph, what does "grew in number" probably mean?	*There were more of them.*
How did you figure out the meaning?	*It sounds like the number grew, which means more plants.*
In the last paragraph, what does "survive" probably mean?	*to live, be healthy*
How did you figure out the meaning?	*It says the plants are still here today, so they must have lived.*
What part of the pitcher plant has a different shape from its ancestors?	*the leaves*
How did the shape change?	*They used to be flatter. Now they are so deep that they look like pitchers or wells.*
How long does it take for a plant to develop new parts or change a lot?	*thousands of years; many, many generations*

Meat-Eating Plants

When you think of meat eaters, you probably don't think of plants. Think again! Most green plants make their own food. Meat-eating plants do, too. But they also need some meat on the menu. Most of these plants grow in weak, swampy soil or even in rocky places. These places no longer give them enough nutrients. To stay healthy, the plants trap and eat insects, spiders, and other small animals. Don't worry—they are not man-eating plants!

Venus' flytrap

The Venus' flytrap grows in North and South Carolina. This deadly plant makes nectar, which attracts bugs. Its leaves have tiny hairs. When a bug moves across the hairs, they snap shut like a trap. The edges of the trap have long, stiff "teeth." The teeth close around the bug. It can't escape. Then special juices break down the bug's body.

The pitcher plant is another meat eater. It grows on every continent except Europe and Antarctica. Sweet-smelling juice collects inside its leafy "pitchers," which look like deep wells. Insects, frogs, and other small animals can't resist this juice. When an animal takes a sip, it falls in. The pitcher has slippery walls. These keep the animal from climbing back out. Before long, the animal turns to soup.

pitcher plant

nectar: a sweet liquid

pitcher: a large container used to serve drinks

  Reading Paired Text • EMC 1373 • © Evan-Moor Corp.

Sundews are found around the world. Tiny hairs on their leaves have sticky, sweet droplets. If a curious insect gets trapped in a droplet, the leaf curls around it. Within five days, the unlucky bug becomes dinner.

sundew plant

How did these plants become meat eaters? Let's look at the pitcher plant. Scientists believe that its ancestors had leaves that were slightly cup shaped. Individuals with the deeper cup-shaped leaves thrived. They made more plants like themselves. Deeper leaves became more common over time. With each generation, the plant leaves were deeper than in the generation before.

At the same time, some of the plants with deeper leaves started to make special juices. The plants with more juices caught more insects and got more nutrients. The plants grew in number. As time went on, plants in later generations became modern pitcher plants.

Over thousands of years, other plants grew different meat-eating parts that helped them survive. Venus' flytraps grew toothy traps. Sundews grew hairs with sticky droplets. All these meat eaters still make food from sunlight and water. But to stay healthy, they sometimes grab an extra bite to eat.

droplets: small drops

Name: _____

Dictionary

Write a sentence using each vocabulary word.

nutrient: something that living things take in to stay healthy

_____

_____

resist: to keep from eating a food or doing a fun thing

_____

_____

ancestor: a family member who lived long ago

_____

_____

individual: a single member of a group

_____

_____

thrive: to be successful; to grow and be healthy; to do well

_____

_____

generation: members of a group that lived at about the same time

_____

_____

Apply Vocabulary

Complete each sentence using a word from the word box.

Word Box

| ancestors | generation | individual |
| nutrients | resist | thrives |

1. My father's _____ came from Russia and settled in
   Alaska in 1804.

2. Miguel loves his new school and _____ in class.

3. Andrea is the most talented _____ in our singing group.

4. I am usually careful when I ride my skateboard, but it's hard to

   _____ going full speed down Twister Hill Road.

5. People take in many _____ when they eat different kinds
   of vegetables.

6. People in my grandparents' _____ did not have
   computers in school.

Write one new sentence. Use a word from the word box.

1. _____

   _____

Answer Questions

Read and answer each question.

1. What probably happened to an ancestor of the sundew plant that did not make sticky droplets?

   Ⓐ It did not trap any insects.

   Ⓑ It found another way to catch insects.

   Ⓒ It moved to a different place.

   Ⓓ It learned to survive without meat.

2. Venus' flytraps catch bugs by using _____.

   Ⓐ deep wells with slippery sides

   Ⓑ traps that have "teeth"

   Ⓒ hairs that have sticky droplets

   Ⓓ curled leaves

3. How does a Venus' flytrap eat an animal that it catches?

   Ⓐ It uses teeth to chew up the animal.

   Ⓑ It uses roots to soak up the animal's juices.

   Ⓒ It stings the animal and waits for its body to break down.

   Ⓓ It makes juice, which breaks down the animal's body.

4. What is missing from the places meat-eating plants live?

   Ⓐ rich nutrients

   Ⓑ swampy soil

   Ⓒ insects

   Ⓓ rocks

5. How did the ancestors of pitcher plants change into meat eaters?

   _____

   _____

   _____

6. Why did it take so long for ancestor plants to become pitcher plants?

   _____

   _____

   _____

Write About It

Think about the three plants in the selection. You will be asked to compare how and what they eat, where they live, and the problems they had. Use the chart below to organize your writing.

Similarities		

Differences		
Venus' flytrap	**Pitcher plant**	**Sundew**

Writing Prompt

On a separate sheet of paper, write three paragraphs to compare how and what meat-eating plants eat, where they live, and the problems they had. Use details from the selection in your response.

Lesson Plan

1. **Introduce the Selection**

   Tell students they will read a selection about a tiger's actions and the effects those actions have on himself and those in his surroundings.

2. **Read Aloud the Selection**

   Reproduce the selection and distribute it to each student. Students will use this for all activities within the unit.

   Have students follow along silently as you read aloud. Direct students' attention to graphic elements or visual aids.

3. **Introduce Vocabulary**

   Reproduce the Dictionary and the Apply Vocabulary activities and distribute them to each student.

   Dictionary: Read aloud the vocabulary words and definitions. Discuss definitions and usage as needed.

   Have students find each vocabulary word in the selection and read the context sentence. Then have students complete <u>one</u> of the leveled activities below:

   • Basic level: Write the context sentence on the lines below its definition.

   • Challenge level: Write a new sentence using the vocabulary word and share the sentence with a partner, a small group, or the whole class.

   Apply Vocabulary: Have students complete the activity independently, with a partner, or in small groups.

4. **Students Read the Selection**

   Have students read the selection independently, with a partner, or in small groups.

5. **Analyze the Selection:**
   Oral Close Reading Activity

   Have students number each paragraph in the selection before they begin the close reading discussion.

   Use the script on the following page to guide students in discussing the selection. Explain that close reading will help them notice important parts of the selection. Encourage students to refer to the selection as necessary to find the information they need.

   To support visual learners, you may wish to cover up the sample responses and reproduce and distribute the discussion questions for students to refer to.

6. **Understand the Selection**

   Reproduce the Answer Questions activity and distribute it to each student. Have students complete the activity independently. Encourage students to refer to the selection as necessary to help them answer the questions and/or to check their answers.

   You may wish to use this as a formative assessment to determine students' understanding of the text.

7. **Write About the Selection**

   Reproduce the Write About It activity and distribute it to each student.

   Graphic Organizer: Have students complete the graphic organizer in small groups.

   Writing Prompt: Have students complete the writing assignment independently on a separate sheet of paper.

Oral Close Reading Activity

Ask students the following text-dependent questions and have them refer to the selection as needed.

Questions	Sample Responses
At the beginning, why could the tiger eat anything he wanted?	*The woods had many animals to eat.*
What phrase from the story tells how much he used to eat?	*"The tiger could fill his belly extra full each day."*
In the second paragraph, which words describe how the tiger felt?	*"hungry," "starving"*
Why was he hungry?	*He had nothing to eat.*
Why couldn't he eat anything?	*He had already eaten up all the animals. He couldn't find any more to eat.*
What did the tiger think when he first saw the jackals?	*He would finally get to eat.*
Look at the last sentence in the third paragraph. Did the jackals shake with fear or run away?	*They ran away.*
Which word in the sentence tells you they did not shake with fear?	*"Instead"*
What idea did one of the jackals have?	*to make the tiger think there was another tiger so he would jump in the well*
How did you figure out what the idea was?	*That's what the jackals did. They described a bigger, faster, louder tiger and said he lived in the well.*
What words did the jackals use to describe the tiger in the hole?	*"bigger," "faster," "he roars louder," "fights harder," "is better than you"*
Why did the jackals describe the other tiger this way?	*to make him sound strong and mean; to make the real tiger want to go after him*
In the eleventh paragraph, what does the word "nervous" mean?	*afraid, scared, worried*
How can you tell?	*It says the tiger didn't want the jackals to think he was afraid, so that must be how he felt.*
How do the illustrations help you understand the story?	*They show what jackals look like, how much bigger the tiger is than the jackals, and how the hole looked to the tiger.*

The Tiger and the Jackals

Once upon a time, a large tiger lived in the woods. He ate whatever he desired. There were many animals around. The tiger could fill his belly extra full each day. The tiger didn't have to work at all to find plenty of food.

One day, the tiger's stomach growled. He realized he was hungry. Even though he looked and looked, he could not find an animal to eat. The tiger had been greedy. Now he was starving all alone in the woods.

The tiger felt worried. He had eaten too much food when he didn't need it. He peeked around every tree, but it looked like there were no animals left. Finally, he saw two jackals. "They sure look tasty!" he thought, and he let out a long, loud roar. But the jackals didn't tremble as the other animals always did. Instead, the jackals ran away.

It had been a long time since the tiger had pursued an animal. Back when the woods were filled with them, he just had to thump them with his large paw. Now, he was running fast and getting close. His belly growled almost as loudly as he did!

One of the jackals had an idea. He whispered to the other one, and they ran into a large bush. They stopped on the other side and stared at the tiger as he came through the bush after them.

"I knew you would stop!" laughed the tiger. "You knew I would catch you!"

"No," said the first jackal, "we stopped because we know something that can stop YOU!"

The tiger snorted and said, "What could possibly stop me?"

"A bigger, faster tiger!" said the second jackal. "He lives on this side of the woods, right over there." The jackals both turned toward a large circle in the ground.

The jackals had seen humans digging the circle. They knew that it went deep into the ground and was filled with water. It was a well, but the tiger didn't know that. "The other tiger lives in that hole," the jackals said. "He roars louder than you and fights harder than you. He is better than you in every way." The jackals looked very serious. They hoped their plan would work.

The tiger was nervous, but he didn't want the jackals to think he was afraid. He walked right up to the edge of the hole and peered inside. He showed his teeth and growled. The other tiger did the same thing! The tiger was scared, but he roared even louder. The other tiger did, too!

"I'm going to fight him first," said the tiger. "Then I am coming back to eat you!" He jumped into the hole and growled all the way down.

The jackals gave a loud howl and danced as they heard the tiger splashing in the well. They knew they were victorious. Soon, there was no sound at all from the well.

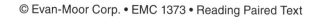

Dictionary

Write a sentence using each vocabulary word.

desire: to want; to long for something

_____

_____

tremble: to shake with fear

_____

_____

pursue: to chase for a long time

_____

_____

peer: to look closely

_____

_____

howl: a loud sound animals make to communicate

_____

_____

victorious: when you win or have a victory; successful

_____

_____

Apply Vocabulary

Complete each sentence using a word from the word box.

Word Box		
desired	howl	peered
pursued	trembles	victorious

1. Marta _____ every time she hears thunder.

2. The _____ soccer team had a pizza party after they won their final game.

3. The police _____ the bank robber until they caught him.

4. I heard a dog give a long _____ after the fire engine went by.

5. What Leo _____ most was to learn to cook.

6. Sue Ann _____ over the fence at the neighbor's new puppy.

Write two new sentences. Use a word from the word box in each.

1. _____

_____

2. _____

_____

Answer Questions

Read and answer each question.

1. The tiger could not find food one day because _____.

   Ⓐ he had eaten too many animals

   Ⓑ all of the animals were hiding

   Ⓒ the jackals had eaten the tiger's food

   Ⓓ another tiger was hunting, too

2. Why did the tiger run after the jackals?

   Ⓐ He was all alone and needed friends.

   Ⓑ He hoped they could lead him to food.

   Ⓒ He wanted help finding another tiger.

   Ⓓ He was hungry and wanted to eat them.

3. Based on their actions, which word best describes the jackals?

   Ⓐ smart

   Ⓑ scared

   Ⓒ useful

   Ⓓ silly

4. What happened to the tiger at the end of the story?

   Ⓐ He ate the two jackals.

   Ⓑ He drowned in the well.

   Ⓒ He caught the tiger in the hole.

   Ⓓ He was killed by the tiger in the well.

5. Describe what the jackals did to trick the tiger.

   _____

   _____

   _____

6. What moral, or lesson, did you learn from this story? Use evidence from the text to support your answer.

   _____

   _____

Write About It

Graphic Organizer

Think about how the woods where the tiger lived had changed. What did the tiger do about the change? You will be asked to explain this change. Use the chart below to organize your writing.

How the woods changed:

How the tiger responded:

The results of the tiger's response:

Writing Prompt

On a separate sheet of paper, write a paragraph to explain how the woods changed and how the tiger responded. Use details from the selection in your response.

Changing with Our Surroundings

Topic: Changing with Our Surroundings
Essential Question: How do living things respond when the environment changes?

Tying It Together

Use the script below to guide students in discussing the essential question and what they have learned about the topic from the paired selections. Feel free to expand on these questions and responses.

To support visual learners, you may wish to cover up the sample responses and reproduce and distribute the discussion questions for students to refer to.

Questions	Sample Responses
What problem were both the tiger and the plants having at first?	*They weren't getting enough food or the right kind of food or nutrients.*
What changes had caused the problems they were having?	*The soil where the plants lived was no longer very good. The tiger had eaten almost all of his food.*
How was the topic "changing with our surroundings" shown in "Meat-Eating Plants"?	*The plants all changed over time to be able to eat meat from bugs or small animals when they couldn't get nutrients from the soil. Each generation changed shape or grew new parts.*
How was the topic "changing with our surroundings" shown in "The Tiger and the Jackals"?	*The tiger liked to eat every animal he could, but he didn't change his habits as the food ran out in his surroundings. He didn't change his behavior when the jackals didn't act like forest animals used to, either.*
Which living things responded better when their environment changed? Why?	*The plants responded better. When they weren't getting nutrients from the soil, they found another way. Each generation of the plants got a little better at changing so that they could eat bugs or small animals. Then they got the right nutrients. They are still alive. The tiger is not.*
Why do you think these selections were paired together?	*They both have to do with a slow change that happens where something lives a long time. One shows you what happens when you find a way to change with your surroundings. The other shows you what happens if you just act the same way and do the same things.*

Plan Your Writing

Graphic Organizer

Think about how the plants in "Meat-Eating Plants" and the tiger in "The Tiger and the Jackals" responded to changes in their surroundings. What problems did they have to overcome? How did they respond to the problems? What was the result of their responses? You will be asked to write about how they responded and how successful they were. Use the chart below to organize your writing.

	Plants	Tiger
Problem		
Response to problem		
Result of response		

Write an Essay

Writing Prompt

Write an essay to compare how the plants in "Meat-Eating Plants" and the tiger in "The Tiger and the Jackals" responded to changes in their surroundings and what the results were. Give your essay a title. Include details from the selections. Use transitions to connect your ideas.

Title: _____

_____

_____

_____

_____

_____

_____

_____

_____

_____

_____

_____

_____

_____

Water, Weather, and Winter

Student Objective:	Students will understand that the water cycle is a repeating pattern and that water on Earth has many uses in all its forms.
Essential Question:	## How does water affect our lives?
Topic Introduction:	Share the unit title and essential question with students. Explain to students that water helps maintain life on Earth. Tell students that they will read two selections about how water affects our lives in different ways through the year.

Paired Text Selections:

Assessment Materials:

Lesson Plan

1. Introduce the Selection

Tell students they will read how water changes and how we use it. Review with students that water occurs in nature in different forms.

2. Read Aloud the Selection

Reproduce the selection and distribute it to each student. Students will use this for all activities within the unit.

Have students follow along silently as you read aloud. Direct students' attention to graphic elements or visual aids.

3. Introduce Vocabulary

Reproduce the Dictionary and the Apply Vocabulary activities and distribute them to each student.

Dictionary: Read aloud the vocabulary words and definitions. Point out that *collect* is a multiple-meaning word, or a homonym. Discuss definitions and usage as needed.

Have students find each vocabulary word in the selection and read the context sentence. Then have students complete <u>one</u> of the leveled activities below:

- Basic level: Write the context sentence on the lines below its definition.

- Challenge level: Write a new sentence using the vocabulary word and share the sentence with a partner, a small group, or the whole class.

Apply Vocabulary: Have students complete the activity independently, with a partner, or in small groups.

4. Students Read the Selection

Have students read the selection independently, with a partner, or in small groups.

5. Analyze the Selection: Oral Close Reading Activity

Have students number each paragraph in the selection before they begin the close reading discussion.

Use the script on the following page to guide students in discussing the selection. Explain that close reading will help them notice important parts of the selection. Encourage students to refer to the selection as necessary to find the information they need.

To support visual learners, you may wish to cover up the sample responses and reproduce and distribute the discussion questions for students to refer to.

6. Understand the Selection

Reproduce the Answer Questions activity and distribute it to each student. Have students complete the activity independently. Encourage students to refer to the selection as necessary to help them answer the questions and/or to check their answers.

You may wish to use this as a formative assessment to determine students' understanding of the text.

7. Write About the Selection

Reproduce the Write About It activity and distribute it to each student.

Graphic Organizer: Have students complete the graphic organizer in small groups.

Writing Prompt: Have students complete the writing assignment independently on a separate sheet of paper.

Oral Close Reading Activity

Ask students the following text-dependent questions and have them refer to the selection as needed.

Questions	Sample Responses
In the second paragraph, what is "invisible water"?	*water that can't be seen*
Where is this water?	*in the air*
What is another name for water in the air?	*water vapor*
If water we cannot see is called "invisible," what would you call water that you *can* see?	*visible*
What causes water to go into the air?	*heat*
Where does the heat come from?	*the sun, a clothes dryer, a stove, your breath, any heat source*
Can water vapor transform into liquid water?	*yes*
Give three examples of this from the selection.	*fogging up a cold window, water droplets on a cold soda can, water droplets on a cold spoon*
What do the surfaces of all three objects have in common?	*They are cold.*
What kinds of vapor can you see?	*fog, steam, clouds*
What forms of water are in clouds?	*tiny drops of liquid water and ice pieces*
Are clouds probably cold or warm?	*cold*
Why are clouds probably cold?	*Vapor turns to liquid when it meets something cold/ ice in clouds means it's probably cold.*
What makes the clouds rain or snow?	*Water and/or ice collects and becomes too heavy to continue floating.*
What do plants do in the water cycle?	*Their roots take in water, and their leaves give off vapor.*
How is this similar to what people do?	*People drink water and breathe out vapor.*
Why do forests get a lot of rain?	*The many trees give off vapor, which makes clouds, which rain on the trees and keep them alive.*

Water All Around Us

If someone asked you to think of water, what would you think of? You might think of something like the ocean, a swimming pool, or a bottle of water. Water is all around us, and we use it for many things. We clean with it, drink it, and water plants with it. We even use water for fun. We swim in it, boat on it, and use it to squirt each other with water pistols. Water is very important, and we see it all around us.

But what about invisible water? Invisible water is all around us, too! The puddles from a windy rainstorm dry up in the sun's heat, even on a cool day. As wet clothes dry out, the water goes away. If you boil a pot of water for a long time, the water disappears. Where does this water go? It goes into the air.

Water that we can see and pour is called liquid water. Water that freezes into ice is called solid water. When water disappears and goes into the air, it is called water vapor. When water is changing from liquid water to water vapor, it is *evaporating*. There is a lot of evaporated water in the air. You can also make water vapor transform back into liquid water. When you breathe on a cold window, the water vapor in your breath fogs up the window glass. The water vapor in the air will turn back into liquid water on the outside of an ice-cold soda can. If you carefully hold a cold spoon over a pot of boiling water, the water vapor will turn back into liquid water on the bottom of the spoon.

Can we ever see water in the air? Most water in the air is invisible, but there are some examples we can see. One example is steam from boiling water. Another is clouds, which are made of billions of tiny drops of liquid water and ice. The drops of water and ice pieces are so small that they can float!

Sometimes, the drops of water in clouds collect, or the ice pieces grow. As the drops of water or ice pieces get bigger, they get too heavy to float and they fall down as rain or snow.

Once the liquid water is back on the ground, does it stop changing? It collects into streams, lakes, oceans, and underground wells. Living things, including people, collect it and use it again. However, the water won't stay on the ground forever. Heat makes water evaporate into water vapor. People and other animals drink liquid water and breathe out water vapor. Plants take in water with their roots and give off water vapor from their leaves. Some of this water vapor stays invisible in the air. Some of it turns back into tiny drops of water and gathers together as a cloud. Some clouds produce rain and become another part of the infinite cycle of water moving around on our beautiful planet.

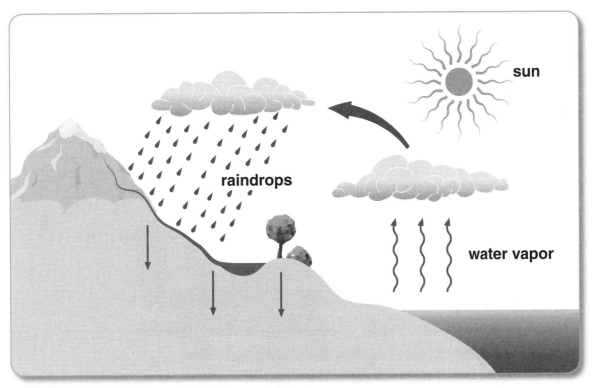

The endless water cycle

Dictionary

Write a sentence using each vocabulary word.

invisible: cannot be seen

_____

_____

liquid: something that is wet and does not have its own shape

_____

_____

transform: to change

_____

_____

collect: to come together and combine into one

_____

_____

infinite: endless

_____

_____

cycle: a series of events that happen over and over

_____

_____

Apply Vocabulary

Complete each sentence using a word from the word box.

Word Box

collected	cycle	infinite
invisible	liquid	transformed

1. Our teacher has an _____ list of ideas for fun math games.

2. Year after year, spring always comes after winter as part of the

   _____ of the seasons.

3. Last Saturday, it was so hot that my cherry snow cone melted into a pink

   _____ before I could finish it.

4. After the rains came, the empty field _____ into a garden
   of wildflowers.

5. The cut on my finger has healed so well that it is now _____.

6. All the neighbors _____ at the Bessants' house to
   discuss the new school crosswalk.

Write one new sentence. Use a word from the word box.

1. _____

   _____

Answer Questions

Read and answer each question.

1. Why do clothes dry faster hanging in the sunlight than in the shade?

   Ⓐ Things move slower in the shade.

   Ⓑ Heat from the sun helps water evaporate.

   Ⓒ It is windier in sunlight than in shade.

   Ⓓ Light causes water to go away.

2. What must happen for rain to fall?

   Ⓐ Ice pieces have to turn into water drops.

   Ⓑ It needs to be very cold outside.

   Ⓒ The water drops have to be too heavy to float.

   Ⓓ The water needs to be invisible in the air.

3. How do plants help form clouds?

   Ⓐ Plants give off water vapor through their leaves.

   Ⓑ Plants put out water through their roots.

   Ⓒ Plants keep water drops from collecting.

   Ⓓ Plants make an area warmer.

4. Which is an example of water evaporating?

   Ⓐ your breath fogging up a window

   Ⓑ wet clothes drying on a clothesline

   Ⓒ rain forming puddles on the ground

   Ⓓ water forming on a cold soda can

5. What is a difference between liquid water and water vapor?

   _____

   _____

   _____

6. Give an example of water vapor transforming back into liquid water.

   _____

   _____

   _____

Write About It

Graphic Organizer

Think about a way you use water. You will be asked to explain how water from a puddle became the water you use. Use the chart below to organize your writing.

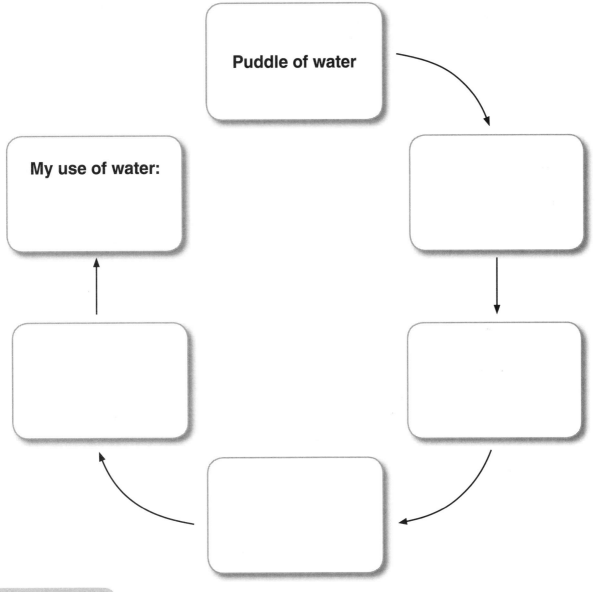

Writing Prompt

On a separate sheet of paper, write three paragraphs to explain how water from a puddle became water that you use. Use details from the selection in your response.

Lesson Plan

1. Introduce the Selection

Tell students that Alaska is in the United States but that it is not connected to the rest of the states. Use a map to show students where Alaska is. Help students pronounce the proper names: Panika [pan-EE-kuh], Kiviaq [KIV-ee-ak], Takotna [tuh-KOT-nuh].

2. Read Aloud the Selection

Reproduce the selection and distribute it to each student. Students will use this for all activities within the unit. Point out that some of the words in the text are defined at the bottom of the pages.

Have students follow along silently as you read aloud. Direct students' attention to graphic elements or visual aids.

3. Introduce Vocabulary

Reproduce the Dictionary and the Apply Vocabulary activities and distribute them to each student.

Dictionary: Read aloud the vocabulary words and definitions. Point out that *can* and *bank* are multiple-meaning words, or homonyms. Discuss definitions and usage as needed.

Have students find each vocabulary word in the selection and read the context sentence. Then have students complete <u>one</u> of the leveled activities below:

- Basic level: Write the context sentence on the lines below its definition.

- Challenge level: Write a new sentence using the vocabulary word and share the sentence with a partner, a small group, or the whole class.

Apply Vocabulary: Have students complete the activity independently, with a partner, or in small groups.

4. Students Read the Selection

Have students read the selection independently, with a partner, or in small groups.

5. Analyze the Selection: Oral Close Reading Activity

Have students number each paragraph in the selection before they begin the close reading discussion.

Use the script on the following page to guide students in discussing the selection. Explain that close reading will help them notice important parts of the selection. Encourage students to refer to the selection as necessary to find the information they need.

To support visual learners, you may wish to cover up the sample responses and reproduce and distribute the discussion questions for students to refer to.

6. Understand the Selection

Reproduce the Answer Questions activity and distribute it to each student. Have students complete the activity independently. Encourage students to refer to the selection as necessary to help them answer the questions and/or to check their answers.

You may wish to use this as a formative assessment to determine students' understanding of the text.

7. Write About the Selection

Reproduce the Write About It activity and distribute it to each student.

Graphic Organizer: Have students complete the graphic organizer in small groups.

Writing Prompt: Have students complete the writing assignment independently on a separate sheet of paper.

Oral Close Reading Activity

Ask students the following text-dependent questions and have them refer to the selection as needed.

Questions	Sample Responses
What are the three Alaska seasons in the selection?	*freeze up/winter, breakup, cleanup*
Which one is Panika's favorite?	*freeze up/winter*
Why does Panika like this season?	*She can do fun things like skate and ski.*
Which one does she like least?	*breakup*
Why doesn't Panika like this season?	*It's very messy/muddy; it causes floods/damage.*
What have Panika's parents been waiting for?	*the river to freeze/the ice road to open*
How can you tell they are excited about it?	*Momma says, "Good news!" and Dad says, "Won't it be great to repair the middle school classroom?"*
What does Kiviaq want to do?	*play basketball*
Why does Momma think the kids in Takotna would like to play basketball with someone else?	*They have also been alone on their side of the river most of the year.*
How do the villagers get around?	*snowmobile and dog sled*
Why doesn't Panika's village have any roads on land?	*The ground is too soft.*
How do the villagers get most of their food?	*hunting and fishing, picking berries*
What kinds of foods do they buy?	*flour, sugar, butter*
In the eighth paragraph, what does the word "overflows" probably mean?	*flow/spill/run over the edge*
How did you figure it out?	*It's a compound word from "over" and "flows," and the water behind the ice goes over the river's edge.*

Panika's Favorite Season

It is said that there are three seasons in Alaska, and they're not like anywhere else. Winter is the *freeze up* season, Panika's favorite. It is dark and cold—sometimes 40 below zero—but her family doesn't mind. Finally Panika and her brother, Kiviaq, can ski to school. Finally Panika gets to ice skate. Finally the sled dogs have snow to run through.

Her parents are happy, too. "Good news!" Momma announced. "The river ice is two feet thick now, so the ice road is open!" The soft ground of their village isn't strong enough to build roads on. But in winter, the rivers freeze deep enough for trucks to drive on and planes to land on.

"I'll order the village fuel and all the lumber for the school," their father said. "Won't it be great to repair the middle school classroom, Kiviaq? I'm sure you'd like to get back with your class."

"That's true, but I haven't minded hanging out with the 'babies,'" Kiviaq teased his sister. Last year, part of the village flooded, and one entire corner of the school was damaged. The middle school class was split up. The sixth-graders moved into the elementary classroom, and the older kids joined the high school class. Kiviaq continued, "What I'm really looking forward to is having the school gym open again. I miss playing basketball."

"With the ice road open, you can take the snowmobile across the river to Takotna," suggested

---

fuel: oil or gas to make heaters and other machines run

lumber: logs or long pieces of wood for building

snowmobile: a small vehicle with an engine that travels across snow

Momma. "I'm sure those kids would love to have someone else to play against."

"Kiviaq may want basketball, but I want blueberry pie," Panika stated. "We haven't had a pie since we ran out of flour and butter back in December." In the remote areas of Alaska, people fish and hunt for most of their food. They dry salmon and moose meat. They also pick gallons of berries. They can the berries to eat later. These dried and canned foods are available through the long winter. They buy only a few other foods, like flour, sugar, and butter, along with household supplies and clothes. These foods and supplies have to be flown to the village.

Three days later, the supply plane landed on the ice road. Panika's whole village was there to greet it. They brought their snowmobiles and dog sleds to haul their goods home. Cars are of no use in a village without roads!

Months later, the ice road started to thaw. Now it was Panika's least favorite season—*breakup*. When the river ice first starts to melt, giant ice chunks collide as they float downstream. They sometimes get stuck going around a bend, and the water behind them overflows the banks.

"Did you wash off the dogs, Panika?" asked her father.

"Yes, but they're already muddy again!" Panika complained. "Why must the whole village become a muddy lake every year?"

And the third Alaska season? *Cleanup!*

Dictionary

Write a sentence using each vocabulary word.

remote: far away from cities or towns

_____

_____

can: to save fresh food in jars or cans to eat later

_____

_____

available: ready to use

_____

_____

haul: to carry something heavy a long way

_____

_____

thaw: to melt or warm up something frozen

_____

_____

collide: to hit, bump, or crash into

_____

_____

bend: a part that is crooked or bent

_____

_____

bank: the edge of a river

_____

_____

Apply Vocabulary

Complete each sentence using a word from the word box.

Word Box			
available	bank	bend	can
collide	haul	remote	thaw

1. Please _____ that heavy trunk to the garage.

2. Uncle Roberto took the cheesecake out of the freezer to

   _____ it for the party.

3. Nadia didn't see the bike until it came around the _____.

4. The lost dog stumbled down the steep _____ into the river.

5. My grandparents _____ plums to enjoy all year long.

6. Our teacher is always _____ after school to help us.

7. When swimmers race, they stay in their own lane so they won't

   _____.

8. The Clarks moved to a _____ island in Maine.

Answer Questions

Read and answer each question.

1. Why does the school need repair?

   Ⓐ It is out of fuel.

   Ⓑ It has frozen shut.

   Ⓒ It has damage from a flood.

   Ⓓ It is too small for middle school.

2. Why hasn't the family had blueberry pie since December?

   Ⓐ They ran out of flour and butter.

   Ⓑ They have been too busy cleaning up mud.

   Ⓒ They couldn't find any more blueberries to pick.

   Ⓓ They prefer to eat salmon and moose meat in winter.

3. What does Panika's father do when the ice road opens?

   Ⓐ plays basketball

   Ⓑ cleans up the mud

   Ⓒ goes skating and skiing

   Ⓓ orders fuel and lumber

4. Why don't the villagers drive cars?

   Ⓐ It is too cold for cars to work.

   Ⓑ There are no roads most of the year.

   Ⓒ There are no other villages to drive to.

   Ⓓ Cars are too heavy to drive on ice.

5. Why is the ice road important to the village?

   _____

   _____

   _____

6. Explain how breakup is different from the spring season in most other places and why.

   _____

   _____

   _____

Name: _____

Write About It

Graphic Organizer

Think about how frozen and melted water were useful to Panika's village and how they were a problem. You will be asked to explain how water was useful and how it caused problems. Use the chart below to organize your writing.

Ways that water was useful	Ways that water was a problem
1.	
2.	
3.	

Writing Prompt

On a separate sheet of paper, write two paragraphs to explain how water was useful and how it caused problems in Panika's village. Use details from the selection in your response.

Water, Weather, and Winter

Topic: Water, Weather, and Winter
Essential Question: How does water affect our lives?

Tying It Together

Use the script below to guide students in discussing the essential question and what they have learned about the topic from the paired selections. Feel free to expand on these questions and responses.

To support visual learners, you may wish to cover up the sample responses and reproduce and distribute the discussion questions for students to refer to.

Questions	Sample Responses
How is liquid water useful?	*You can drink it, wash things and grow plants with it, bathe, swim, fish, play in it.*
How is frozen water useful?	*You can skate and ski on it and walk, drive, or land a plane on it if it is thick enough.*
How can water cause problems?	*It can cause floods, damage buildings, make things dirty/messy/muddy.*
Think about what causes evaporation. Why is there little evaporation during freeze up, and how does this affect the weather?	*Heat causes evaporation. Since it is really cold in winter, there isn't much heat or evaporation, so there isn't much water in the air. Without water vapor, there aren't many clouds or much rain, so the weather is dry but cold.*
How does water affect your life? What are things you can or can't do because of water?	*Answers will vary. Encourage students to think beyond the actual water use to other results, such as taking a ferry boat to visit a friend across a river.*
How was the topic "water, weather, and winter" shown in "Water All Around Us"?	*It described where water is and all its forms, how hot weather causes evaporation and clouds cause rainy weather, and that winter snow and ice are water, too.*
How was the topic "water, weather, and winter" shown in "Panika's Favorite Season"?	*In winter, the weather gets cold enough so the water freezes the river and the villagers can do things they can't do at other times.*
Why do you think these selections were paired together?	*They both talk about different forms of water. One tells how it changes form and moves in a cycle and the other tells how it affects a village in surprising ways, like what they can eat and when they can play basketball.*

Plan Your Writing

Think about the part, or stage, of the water cycle where rain falls. Also think about the breakup season in Alaska. You will be asked to compare what happens during the rain stage of the water cycle with what happens during breakup. Use the chart below to organize your writing.

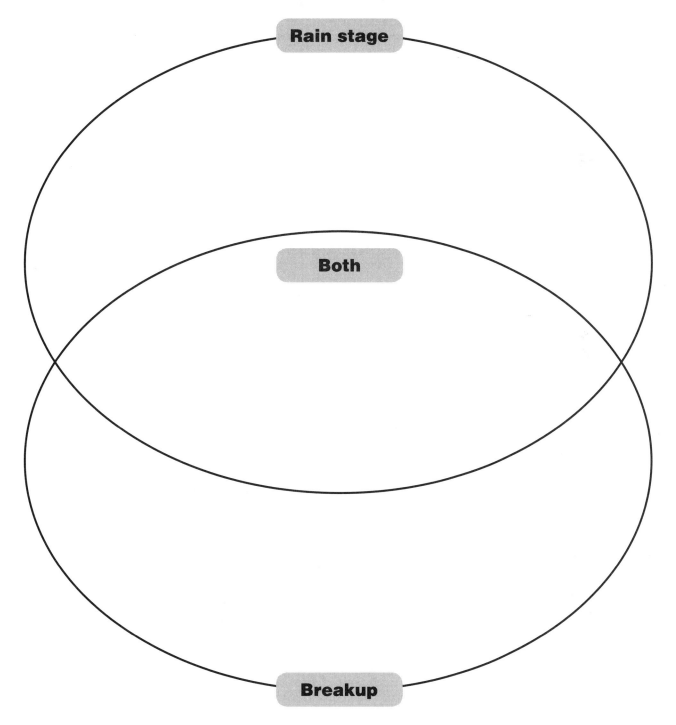

Write an Essay

Write an essay to compare how the rain stage of the water cycle is similar to and different from breakup. Give your essay a title. Include details from the selections. Use transitions to connect your ideas.

Title: _____

_____

_____

_____

_____

_____

_____

_____

_____

_____

_____

_____

_____

Observing Our World and Beyond

Student Objective: Students will understand that people use tools and their senses to collect and analyze information to increase their knowledge of the world.

Essential Question:

How do we learn our place in the universe?

Topic Introduction: Share the unit title and essential question with students. Then explain to students that people learn new things in many ways. Sometimes we learn from others, but some things have to be figured out for the first time. Tell students they will read two selections about making discoveries.

Paired Text Selections:

Assessment Materials:

Lesson Plan

1. Introduce the Selection

Tell students they will read about making discoveries. Review with students that Earth is one of eight planets in our solar system which also includes the sun and the moon that circles Earth.

2. Read Aloud the Selection

Reproduce the selection and distribute it to each student. Students will use this for all activities within the unit. Point out that some of the words in the text are defined at the bottom of the pages.

Have students follow along silently as you read aloud. Direct students' attention to graphic elements or visual aids.

3. Introduce Vocabulary

Reproduce the Dictionary and the Apply Vocabulary activities and distribute them to each student.

Dictionary: Read aloud the vocabulary words and definitions. Discuss definitions and usage as needed.

Have students find each vocabulary word in the selection and read the context sentence. Then have students complete <u>one</u> of the leveled activities below:

- Basic level: Write the context sentence on the lines below its definition.

- Challenge level: Write a new sentence using the vocabulary word and share the sentence with a partner, a small group, or the whole class.

Apply Vocabulary: Have students complete the activity independently, with a partner, or in small groups.

4. Students Read the Selection

Have students read the selection independently, with a partner, or in small groups.

5. Analyze the Selection: Oral Close Reading Activity

Have students number each paragraph in the selection before they begin the close reading discussion.

Use the script on the following page to guide students in discussing the selection. Explain that close reading will help them notice important parts of the selection. Encourage students to refer to the selection as necessary to find the information they need.

To support visual learners, you may wish to cover up the sample responses and reproduce and distribute the discussion questions for students to refer to.

6. Understand the Selection

Reproduce the Answer Questions activity and distribute it to each student. Have students complete the activity independently. Encourage students to refer to the selection as necessary to help them answer the questions and/or to check their answers.

You may wish to use this as a formative assessment to determine students' understanding of the text.

7. Write About the Selection

Reproduce the Write About It activity and distribute it to each student.

Graphic Organizer: Have students complete the graphic organizer in small groups.

Writing Prompt: Have students complete the writing assignment independently on a separate sheet of paper.

Oral Close Reading Activity

Ask students the following text-dependent questions and have them refer to the selection as needed.

Questions	Sample Responses
In the first paragraph, what does the word "theories" probably mean?	*ideas, what we think*
How can you tell?	*It says we test them, and then it talks about testing ideas.*
What causes science to change?	*We get more information, we learn from experiments.*
How do tools help change what we know?	*They help us gather information, see things we can't see just by looking with our eyes alone.*
What tool did Galileo invent?	*the telescope*
How did he get the idea for the telescope?	*He heard about a spyglass and made it better.*
What information do the illustrations give you?	*The first telescope looked like a long tube, it wasn't very big, you can hold it or rest it on a stand, you put the smaller end close to your eye.*
In the third paragraph, why is the phrase "were distinctly seen as if nearby" in quotation marks?	*It is a phrase that someone said.*
Who said it?	*the man in Holland who invented the spyglass*
What were the first things Galileo discovered after he started looking into space with his telescope?	*The moon has mountains and craters, the Milky Way is made of stars, and Jupiter has four moons.*
What did people in the 1600s believe about the position of the sun, moon, and Earth?	*They thought the sun and moon moved around Earth.*
Why did they think that?	*They saw the sun and moon rise and set in the sky every day, they couldn't feel Earth moving.*
Who was the first person to think that Earth revolves around the sun?	*Copernicus*
Why didn't everyone believe him?	*He couldn't prove it, and it went against what people already believed.*
How did Galileo use a telescope to prove that Copernicus was right?	*He saw changes in how Venus looked that showed it wasn't circling Earth.*

New Invention, New Universe

Things are always changing. In nature, volcanoes create new land, and caterpillars change into butterflies. People change, too. Children grow into adults, and athletes get stronger. Science also changes. As we gather more information and test our theories, we better understand how things work. One way to gather more information is to use tools. Microscopes and X-rays are examples of science tools.

One scientist who helped change our understanding of the world and our place in the universe was Galileo Galilei. He was born in Italy in 1564. Galileo's father wanted him to be a doctor. However, Galileo liked math, and he became a mathematics teacher. At that time, almost everyone assumed that heavy objects fall faster. Galileo decided to experiment. Legend has it that he dropped balls of different weights from the Leaning Tower of Pisa. Surprisingly, the light ball fell just as fast as the heavy ball. This forced people to change their beliefs.

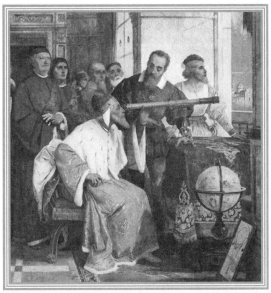

Galileo presents his first telescope to the leader of Venice.

Galileo heard about a new invention called a spyglass. A man in Holland had put eyeglass lenses in a tube. He found that things that were far away "were distinctly seen as if nearby." You can see this by looking through some eyeglasses. As you move the lenses farther away from your eyes, the image size changes.

microscopes: tools that make tiny things visible

lenses: curved pieces of glass that make things look bigger

Galileo took that idea and created a telescope that magnified things to look three times as big. Later, he created even more powerful telescopes.

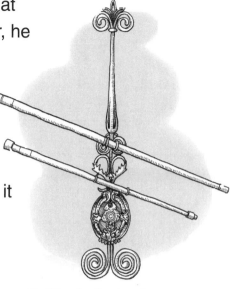

Galileo's first telescopes on display

Galileo learned many new things by looking at the stars and planets with his new tool. First, he proved that the surface of the moon had mountains and craters, just like Earth. Before his discovery, people believed that it was perfectly smooth. Next, he discovered that the Milky Way was made of stars. After that, he noticed that Jupiter had four moons moving around it. This led Galileo to prove something that challenged a strong belief of that time. In the 1600s, most people thought that everything, including the sun, moved around Earth. After all, Earth doesn't feel like it is moving. Also, the sun and planets look like they are moving around us. Seeing moons revolve around Jupiter proved that not everything circled Earth. Through his telescope, Galileo saw that there were changes in the appearance of Venus's size and shape. These changes would be impossible if Venus circled Earth.

The idea that Earth revolved around the sun was not new. A man named Nicolaus Copernicus thought of this idea 60 years before. However, Galileo's telescope provided the first proof that Copernicus was right—Earth was not the center of the universe. Who would have thought that such a small tool could make such a big change in our knowledge and understanding!

crater: a large, bowl-shaped hole in the ground

Dictionary

Write a sentence using each vocabulary word.

create: to make

_____

_____

tool: something that helps you do work or learn

_____

_____

assume: to believe

_____

_____

experiment: to test an idea in a controlled way

_____

_____

distinctly: clearly

_____

_____

image: what you see through a lens on a screen

_____

_____

magnify: to make bigger

_____

_____

challenge: to question an idea

_____

_____

Apply Vocabulary

Complete each sentence using a word from the word box.

Word Box

assumed	challenged	created	distinctly
experiment	image	magnified	tools

1. We needed some special _____ to put the new bicycle together.

2. After I dropped my computer, the _____ on the screen was a little fuzzy.

3. Lupe decided to _____ with making a new kind of soup.

4. I _____ heard Mr. Mori say that there is a test tomorrow.

5. After the ocean washed away the old one, I _____ a very different kind of sand castle.

6. When our teacher showed us the map, the projector _____ it so the back row of students could see it better.

7. He _____ that Alison was always correct, but sometimes she made mistakes.

8. Terry didn't think the team's solution to the problem would work, so she

   _____ it.

Answer Questions

Read and answer each question.

1. In Galileo Galilei's time, what did most people assume about how objects fall?

   Ⓐ They said falling objects are lighter than those on the ground.

   Ⓑ They were sure that everything falls at the same speed.

   Ⓒ They believed that objects become heavier as they fall.

   Ⓓ They thought heavy things fall faster than lighter things.

2. What important idea did Nicolaus Copernicus think of?

   Ⓐ Earth revolves around the sun.

   Ⓑ Jupiter has moons that circle it.

   Ⓒ Earth's moon has mountains.

   Ⓓ The Milky Way is made of stars.

3. Galileo's telescope helped prove that almost nothing circles Earth. This is because the telescope allowed people to see _____.

   Ⓐ the center of the universe

   Ⓑ craters on Earth's moon

   Ⓒ moons circling Jupiter

   Ⓓ Earth circling Venus

4. Which of these best explains why Galileo is important in history?

   Ⓐ He taught mathematics.

   Ⓑ He did experiments by dropping objects.

   Ⓒ He saw that the Milky Way was made of stars.

   Ⓓ He made discoveries that changed what people thought.

5. How was the spyglass made? What did it do?

   _____

   _____

6. Do you think Galileo believed that Earth revolved around the sun? Use examples from the selection to support your answer.

   _____

   _____

   _____

Write About It

Graphic Organizer

Think about the things that Galileo Galilei learned with his telescope that were surprising to the people of his time. You will be asked to describe some of those discoveries and explain how they changed people's beliefs. Use the chart below to organize your writing.

What Galileo learned	How beliefs changed
1.	
2.	
3.	

Writing Prompt

On a separate sheet of paper, write three paragraphs to explain how Galileo's discoveries changed people's beliefs. Include details from the selection in your response.

Lesson Plan

1. Introduce the Selection

Tell students they will read a science fiction selection that takes place on the International Space Station, called the ISS for short. The ISS is a real science research station that circles above Earth.

2. Read Aloud the Selection

Reproduce the selection and distribute it to each student. Students will use this for all activities within the unit. Point out that some of the words in the text are defined at the bottom of the pages.

Have students follow along silently as you read aloud. Direct students' attention to graphic elements or visual aids.

3. Introduce Vocabulary

Reproduce the Dictionary and the Apply Vocabulary activities and distribute them to each student.

Dictionary: Read aloud the vocabulary words and definitions. Point out that *switch* is a multiple-meaning word, or a homonym. Discuss definitions and usage as needed.

Have students find each vocabulary word in the selection and read the context sentence. Then have students complete <u>one</u> of the leveled activities below:

- Basic level: Write the context sentence on the lines below its definition.

- Challenge level: Write a new sentence using the vocabulary word and share the sentence with a partner, a small group, or the whole class.

Apply Vocabulary: Have students complete the activity independently, with a partner, or in small groups.

4. Students Read the Selection

Have students read the selection independently, with a partner, or in small groups.

5. Analyze the Selection: Oral Close Reading Activity

Have students number each paragraph in the selection before they begin the close reading discussion.

Use the script on the following page to guide students in discussing the selection. Explain that close reading will help them notice important parts of the selection. Encourage students to refer to the selection as necessary to find the information they need.

To support visual learners, you may wish to cover up the sample responses and reproduce and distribute the discussion questions for students to refer to.

6. Understand the Selection

Reproduce the Answer Questions activity and distribute it to each student. Have students complete the activity independently. Encourage students to refer to the selection as necessary to help them answer the questions and/or to check their answers.

You may wish to use this as a formative assessment to determine students' understanding of the text.

7. Write About the Selection

Reproduce the Write About It activity and distribute it to each student.

Graphic Organizer: Have students complete the graphic organizer in small groups.

Writing Prompt: Have students complete the writing assignment independently on a separate sheet of paper.

Oral Close Reading Activity

Ask students the following text-dependent questions and have them refer to the selection as needed.

Questions	Sample Responses
When does this story take place?	*in the future*
How can you tell?	*Rhea and her family live in space, she floats down the hall, she uses computer equipment that hasn't been made yet.*
In the second paragraph, what does the word "orbits" probably mean?	*travels/flies around*
How can you tell?	*It says the ISS is orbiting Earth and that it is passing over Chicago. The Earth-viewing camera makes it sound like they can see different parts of Earth at different times.*
Where does Diana live?	*on Earth, near Chicago*
What are two ways Rhea sees what the Chicago area looks like?	*She looks out the viewing window, and she sees it on her computer screen.*
What does she see in both views?	*the lake*
Why does it look different in each view?	*One is from far away, the other is close up.*
What words does the author use to describe how Rhea moves around on the ISS?	*"floated," "glided," "coasted"*
Why did the author use these words instead of "move"?	*They are more interesting; they tell how she moved— softly, gently, smoothly, easily, not quickly.*
What do Rhea's parents do on the ISS?	*They are scientists.*
How can you tell?	*They run tests and use equipment to study material and weather.*
Who is Titan?	*the Internet, Rhea's computer*
What did Titan do for Rhea?	*responded to voice commands, went to SpaceBook to connect her with Diana using video chat, identified and described objects, answered questions*
What kind of information can't Titan provide?	*how things feel*

SpaceBook Friends

At 8:00 a.m., Rhea's mother appeared on Rhea's bedroom wall. "Time to get up, sweetie," she said. Rhea mumbled good morning. Then she unzipped her soft bed bag. She grabbed her computer headset and floated out of the room. She was excited to see her friend Diana today.

Diana lives nearly 250 miles away, in another world. Diana lives on planet Earth, near a city named Chicago. Rhea lives in outer space, high above Earth. Her home is the International Space Station, called the ISS for short. The ISS orbits Earth so quickly that its location changes every second. Rhea's parents were born on the ISS, and so was she. Her father works in the chemical lab, running tests on samples of materials from Mars and Venus to figure out what they are. Her mother studies how space and the atmosphere affect Earth's weather.

Rhea glided down long hallways and coasted into the observation lab. Passing the telescopes, she peered out the large Earth-viewing window. "Hey! We're right over Chicago," said Rhea. The city was easy to identify from space. Its streets formed straight lines that crossed like the lines on a checkerboard, and there was a huge blue patch next to it.

Rhea adjusted her computer headset, moving the screen's arm down, and spoke to it. "Titan, go to SpaceBook, call Diana, and switch on the camera." As fast as a

atmosphere: the air around Earth

shooting star, a 3D scene appeared on the tiny screen in front of Rhea's right eye.

"Hey, Diana!" said Rhea. Diana smiled and waved at the watch she wore on her wrist as Rhea's face appeared.

"Hang on a minute," said Diana as she made her way down a hill that had no trees or grass. Rhea wrinkled her forehead. She tapped twice on the bare hill and said, "Titan, please define this object."

Titan replied, "The object is a mound made up of very small grains of sand. It is called a sand dune."

Rhea observed as Diana's feet dug deep dents into the sand. Clumps of sand flew with every step she took. When she swayed, she used her arms for balance. She could not go fast. "Hmmm," thought Rhea, "sand looks smooth and solid, but it's soft and it gives way when pressed."

The dune ended at the shore of a lake. "I've got to cool off," Diana said. "Then we can talk." Rhea watched as her friend tugged off her shoes and socks and waded into the lake. She heard Diana giggle as she splashed herself with the cool water.

Rhea glanced at her own feet. She always wore socks. Most of the time, her feet did not touch the floor of the ISS, except when she exercised at the gravity gym. She could walk up the walls and across the ceiling, but she had never felt sand squish through her toes. Because she used wet towels to wash, she had never splashed in water, either.

"Titan, tell me how to get to Earth," commanded Rhea.

Dictionary

Write a sentence using each vocabulary word.

location: the place where something is

_____

_____

sample: a small amount of something to test

_____

_____

switch: to turn something on

_____

_____

wrinkle: to move something so it has small folds

_____

_____

bare: plain, without anything on it

_____

_____

grain: a tiny piece of something

_____

_____

sway: to move gently back and forth

_____

_____

Name: _____

Apply Vocabulary

Complete each sentence using a word from the word box.

> **Word Box**
>
> bare   grain   location   sample
>
> sway   switch   wrinkle

1. A _____ of salt is not too heavy for an ant to carry.

2. I circled the _____ of your street on my map.

3. A bad odor made Oscar _____ his nose.

4. Press the red button to _____ on the television.

5. The deer gobbled the flower petals and left the stems _____ .

6. The swing began to _____ as a breeze blew.

7. The doctor took a _____ from the back of my mouth to
   see what is causing my sore throat.

Write two new sentences. Use a word from the word box in each.

1. _____

   _____

2. _____

   _____

Answer Questions

Read and answer each question.

1. Which statement would the author agree with?

    Ⓐ Living on the ISS is very difficult.

    Ⓑ People cannot live in outer space for very long.

    Ⓒ Using a computer is the only way to learn things.

    Ⓓ You can learn by observing carefully.

2. Why does Rhea want to go to Earth?

    Ⓐ She misses her home planet.

    Ⓑ She wants to walk on ceilings and walls.

    Ⓒ She wants to try things that Diana enjoys.

    Ⓓ She wants to see how Earth and the ISS are similar.

3. Which of these is a difference between Rhea and Diana?

    Ⓐ Rhea always wears socks, and Diana never does.

    Ⓑ Rhea can see Diana, but Diana cannot see Rhea.

    Ⓒ Rhea is an alien, and Diana is a human being.

    Ⓓ Rhea lives indoors, but Diana is free to go outdoors.

4. Rhea wrinkled her forehead because she was _____.

    Ⓐ jealous

    Ⓑ puzzled

    Ⓒ excited

    Ⓓ upset

5. What events and details in the story tell you it is science fiction?

    _____

    _____

    _____

6. Why do Rhea's feet rarely touch the floor of the ISS?

    _____

    _____

Write About It

Graphic Organizer

Think about how Rhea and her parents get information. You will be asked to describe different ways of getting information. Include examples of details that Rhea learned about Earth. Use the chart below to organize your writing.

Ways to get information	What Rhea learned about Earth
1.	
2.	
3.	

Writing Prompt

On a separate sheet of paper, write three paragraphs explaining how Rhea and her parents get information and what Rhea learned about Earth. Include details from the selection in your response.

Observing Our World and Beyond

Tying It Together

Topic: Observing Our World and Beyond
Essential Question: How do we learn our place in the universe?

Use the script below to guide students in discussing the essential question and what they have learned about the topic from the paired selections. Feel free to expand on these questions and responses.

To support visual learners, you may wish to cover up the sample responses and reproduce and distribute the discussion questions for students to refer to.

Questions	Sample Responses
What belief did Galileo's telescope help change?	*He proved the sun and planets did not revolve around Earth; Earth and other planets revolve around the sun.*
What belief did Rhea's video camera change?	*Sand is not smooth and solid; it is soft and makes dents when you walk on it.*
What are different ways we learn our place in the universe?	*using science tools; making observations; doing experiments; using computers; asking questions; studying other planets, space, and the atmosphere*
How would Rhea's life have been different without Galileo's discoveries?	*Her family wouldn't live on the ISS or travel in space. Her father wouldn't study materials from other planets.*
How was the topic "observing our world and beyond" shown in "New Invention, New Universe"?	*It told how a famous scientist figured out things that no one else knew or believed. He invented a tool to make things in space look big enough to watch and see how they moved. That told him other details about planets.*
How was the topic "observing our world and beyond" shown in "SpaceBook Friends"?	*It showed how even kids can learn things about Earth and space by observing, using a computer, and asking questions. Rhea's parents also learned things in the science lab where they worked.*
Why do you think these selections were paired together?	*They both describe learning about space, but one gives history and the other is in the future. There are many things in both selections that we do now, such as using computers, observing things, and doing experiments.*

Plan Your Writing

Graphic Organizer

Think about how important the telescope and the computer have been as science tools. You will be asked to decide which one has been more useful for making science discoveries and to support your opinion. Use the chart below to organize your writing.

	What was learned	Why it is important
Telescope		
Computer		

Write an Essay

Writing Prompt

Decide whether the telescope or computer has been a more useful science tool. Write an essay to support your opinion. Give your essay a title. Include details from the selections. Use transitions to connect your ideas.

Title: _____

_____

_____

_____

_____

_____

_____

_____

_____

_____

_____

_____

_____

Growing Up, Growing Strong

Student Objective:

Students will understand that living things grow in different ways and that they need different things in their environments to help them grow.

Essential Question:

What affects how we grow?

Topic Introduction:

Share the unit title and the essential question with students. Explain to students that living things grow. Tell students they will read two selections about how different things affect how living things grow in their environments.

Paired Text Selections:

Assessment Materials:

Lesson Plan

1. Introduce the Selection

Tell students that all living things grow and develop, but it doesn't happen just because they get older. Review with students how the force of gravity pulls things to the ground.

2. Read Aloud the Selection

Reproduce the selection and distribute it to each student. Students will use this for all activities within the unit. Point out that some of the words in the text are defined at the bottom of the pages.

Have students follow along silently as you read aloud. Direct students' attention to graphic elements or visual aids.

3. Introduce Vocabulary

Reproduce the Dictionary and the Apply Vocabulary activities and distribute them to each student.

Dictionary: Read aloud the vocabulary words and definitions. Discuss definitions and usage as needed.

Have students find each vocabulary word in the selection and read the context sentence. Then have students complete <u>one</u> of the leveled activities below:

• Basic level: Write the context sentence on the lines below its definition.

• Challenge level: Write a new sentence using the vocabulary word and share the sentence with a partner, a small group, or the whole class.

Apply Vocabulary: Have students complete the activity independently, with a partner, or in small groups.

4. Students Read the Selection

Have students read the selection independently, with a partner, or in small groups.

5. Analyze the Selection:
Oral Close Reading Activity

Have students number each paragraph in the selection before they begin the close reading discussion.

Use the script on the following page to guide students in discussing the selection. Explain that close reading will help them notice important parts of the selection. Encourage students to refer to the selection as necessary to find the information they need.

To support visual learners, you may wish to cover up the sample responses and reproduce and distribute the discussion questions for students to refer to.

6. Understand the Selection

Reproduce the Answer Questions activity and distribute it to each student. Have students complete the activity independently. Encourage students to refer to the selection as necessary to help them answer the questions and/or to check their answers.

You may wish to use this as a formative assessment to determine students' understanding of the text.

7. Write About the Selection

Reproduce the Write About It activity and distribute it to each student.

Graphic Organizer: Have students complete the graphic organizer in small groups.

Writing Prompt: Have students complete the writing assignment independently on a separate sheet of paper.

Oral Close Reading Activity

Ask students the following text-dependent questions and have them refer to the selection as needed.

Questions	Sample Responses
What is gravity?	*a force that pulls things to the ground*
In the first paragraph, what does it mean that you would feel "weightless"?	*You would feel like you don't weigh anything.*
How did you figure out the meaning?	*"Less" means "without," so "without weight" means you don't have any weight.*
What danger does someone with thin bones face?	*Their bones can break more easily.*
How does the sun affect our bones?	*It helps our bodies make vitamin D.*
What else is needed for vitamin D to be useful?	*calcium*
What kinds of activities make you push against gravity?	*standing, walking, running, jumping, climbing*
Why are jumping and climbing harder to do?	*You have to push or pull yourself off the ground.*
How do the tight rubber straps help astronauts exercise in space?	*They pull the astronaut down onto the exercise equipment so he or she won't float off and can push against the machine.*
Why did the author suggest listening to your heartbeat while lying down and standing up?	*to show us how the heart reacts to gravity*
What happens to astronauts who are in space a long time?	*Their bones lose thickness/get thinner. Their heart and other muscles weaken. Their heart shrinks.*

Growing with Gravity

Have you ever wondered how it would feel to be in space? You would feel mostly weightless because Earth's gravity would not pull you to the ground. You could fly through the air like Superman. You could move heavy equipment with just your fingertips. But it wouldn't mean that you were strong, and it wouldn't help you grow. To grow strong and function properly, many parts of our body require gravity.

Bones are a good example. Gravity, along with several other things, makes bones thick. With gravity's help, calcium makes your bones strong so they won't break easily. As you get older, calcium helps your existing bones grow. Bones absorb calcium from your food with the help of vitamin D, which the sun helps our bodies produce. Astronauts in space actually lose bone thickness because they do not get vitamin D from sunlight, and their bodies do not get to react to gravity.

calcium: a nutrient in milk, salmon, and leafy greens

Your muscles also grow strong because of gravity. Every time you stand, walk, or run, your muscles push back against gravity. When you jump rope or climb, your muscles push back against gravity even more. These kinds of activities may be hard work, but your muscles adapt and grow stronger. In the weightlessness of space, astronauts' muscles get weaker. Astronauts use tight rubber straps to keep themselves attached to their exercise equipment. However, the straps do not pull as well as gravity does.

Your heart is a muscle that responds to gravity, too. Your heart pushes the blood around your body. When you stand, your heart has to work harder to push the blood up to your head. That's because your heart is working against gravity, which pulls your blood down toward your feet. Listen to your heartbeat when you are lying down and again when you stand up. Your heart will probably beat faster when you are standing. When astronauts first go into space, too much blood gets pushed toward their head. Eventually, the heart relaxes and pumps less blood. If an astronaut stayed in space a really long time, the heart would shrink and weaken. Then it would not do its job very well back on Earth.

Being in space would certainly be fun. However, you could not stay for a long time. You have some important growing to do here on Earth. It's time to do some walking, running, climbing, and jumping to get your bones and muscles strong with the help of gravity!

Dictionary

Write a sentence using each vocabulary word.

function: to work

_____

_____

existing: already there

_____

_____

absorb: to soak up

_____

_____

react: to do something in response

_____

_____

activity: a thing to do, often using movement

_____

_____

adapt: to change or improve to work better

_____

_____

relax: to become looser or more calm

_____

_____

Apply Vocabulary

Complete each sentence using a word from the word box.

Word Box
absorbed   activities   adapt   existing
functioning   reacted   relaxed

1. When the school year started, it took me a week to _____ to getting up earlier.

2. My parents thought the _____ fish tank was big enough and that I didn't need a new one.

3. During the fire drill, the class _____ calmly by lining up and leaving the school building.

4. Of all the _____ that we did in camp, I liked rowing the best.

5. His grip on his mother's hand _____ after the scary ride was over.

6. The freezer was not _____ well, and the ice cream melted.

7. The sponge _____ most of the milk Anna spilled.

Write one new sentence. Use a word from the word box.

1. _____

_____

Answer Questions

Read and answer each question.

1. Someone who does not get much
   exercise will probably have _____.

   Ⓐ thinner bones

   Ⓑ more bones

   Ⓒ thicker bones

   Ⓓ fewer bones

2. How does gravity affect the heart?

   Ⓐ It makes the heart wear out
      sooner.

   Ⓑ It pushes blood from the heart to
      the head.

   Ⓒ It gives the heart more exercise.

   Ⓓ It helps the heart absorb more
      vitamin D.

3. Earth's gravity helps _____.

   Ⓐ give bones calcium

   Ⓑ make muscles strong

   Ⓒ get vitamin D from food

   Ⓓ make things easier to move

4. What should astronauts do to help
   their bones while they are in space?

   Ⓐ jump rope really fast

   Ⓑ climb the walls of the space
      station

   Ⓒ move heavy objects around

   Ⓓ use straps on an exercise
      machine

5. In some places in Earth's far north, the sun does not rise for over two months in
   winter. People who live in these areas can easily get thinner bones. Explain why,
   using details from the selection.

   _____

   _____

   _____

6. Give two reasons why changes happen to the bones of an astronaut who has been
   in space a long time.

   _____

   _____

   _____

Write About It

Graphic Organizer

If astronauts were to travel to Mars, they would be in a weightless environment for about seven months. Think about how that trip would affect the astronauts. You will be asked to explain what changes would happen in their bodies, what they could do to keep their bodies as strong as possible, and what would be difficult for them working in Mars's gravity. Use the chart below to organize your writing.

	Main ideas	Supporting details
Changes during travel		
Keeping bodies strong		
Working on Mars		

Writing Prompt

On a separate sheet of paper, write three paragraphs to explain how traveling to Mars would affect astronauts during the long trip and while working on Mars. Include what they could do to keep their bodies as strong as possible. Include details from the selection in your response.

Lesson Plan

1. **Introduce the Selection**

   Tell students they will read a poem about how a bean seed grows into a plant with help from its environment.

2. **Read Aloud the Selection**

   Reproduce the selection and distribute it to each student. Students will use this for all activities within the unit.

   Have students follow along silently as you read aloud. Direct students' attention to graphic elements or visual aids.

3. **Introduce Vocabulary**

   Reproduce the Dictionary and the Apply Vocabulary activities and distribute them to each student.

   Dictionary: Read aloud the vocabulary words and definitions. Point out that *might* is a multiple-meaning word, or a homonym. Discuss definitions and usage as needed.

   Have students find each vocabulary word in the selection and read the context sentence. Then have students complete <u>one</u> of the leveled activities below:

   • Basic level: Write the context sentence on the lines below its definition.

   • Challenge level: Write a new sentence using the vocabulary word and share the sentence with a partner, a small group, or the whole class.

   Apply Vocabulary: Have students complete the activity independently, with a partner, or in small groups.

4. **Students Read the Selection**

   Have students read the selection independently, with a partner, or in small groups.

5. **Analyze the Selection: Oral Close Reading Activity**

   Have students number each stanza in the poem before they begin the close reading discussion.

   Use the script on the following page to guide students in discussing the selection. Explain that close reading will help them notice important parts of the selection. Encourage students to refer to the selection as necessary to find the information they need.

   To support visual learners, you may wish to cover up the sample responses and reproduce and distribute the discussion questions for students to refer to.

6. **Understand the Selection**

   Reproduce the Answer Questions activity and distribute it to each student. Have students complete the activity independently. Encourage students to refer to the selection as necessary to help them answer the questions and/or to check their answers.

   You may wish to use this as a formative assessment to determine students' understanding of the text.

7. **Write About the Selection**

   Reproduce the Write About It activity and distribute it to each student.

   Graphic Organizer: Have students complete the graphic organizer in small groups.

   Writing Prompt: Have students complete the writing assignment independently on a separate sheet of paper.

Oral Close Reading Activity

Ask students the following text-dependent questions and have them refer to the selection as needed.

Questions	Sample Responses
What kind of seed did the narrator plant?	bean
What details helped you figure out that the seed received water and sun?	The bean was "in the moist, warm earth." Moist soil has water. Warm soil means the sun warmed it. Also, the fourth stanza mentions "water underground," and the fifth and seventh stanzas mention "light."
Do you think the seed actually slept the same way you sleep at night?	no
How did the seed sleep?	The seed just lay still under the ground for a long time, until it could begin to grow into a plant.
In stanza 2, what does "underfoot" mean?	under the ground
How did you figure out the meaning?	This is a compound word made from "under" and "foot." You plant a seed under the ground. The seed was "in the moist, warm earth," so it was underground.
Why does the stem grow up?	It likes sunlight.
Why do the roots grow down?	They collect water and nutrients from the soil.
In stanza 6, what does "seed coat" mean?	the cover of a seed that protects it
How did you figure out the meaning?	The illustration shows the shell of the seed falling away. Also, when I wear a coat, it protects me.
How do the green beans grow?	up slender poles
Why does the narrator help the plants grow on slender poles?	The beans will be easier to see that way; the vines of the plant are long, and they climb up the pole.
What will the plant produce?	green beans
What is the narrator planning to do with the green beans?	The narrator will pick the beans for Mom, who will make a green bean casserole with them.
How do the illustrations help you understand the poem?	They show the different stages of the bean plant's growth, and I can see the roots, stem, and seed. I also understand how the plant grows both up and down.

Lean Green Beans

I planted a bean seed
With all that's necessary.
Now the plant grows up and down.
I know this sounds contrary.

My bean seed, in the moist, warm earth,
Slept quietly underfoot.
Then one day the seed awoke.
Out came a tender root.

Smaller roots began to sprout
From the bigger one.
Tiny fingers reaching down,
The work had just begun.

The roots collected nutrients
And water underground.
At this time, a stem took shape.
But it did not reach down.

No, instead the stem reached up
And headed toward the light.
It lifted out the little seed
And stretched with all its might.

Soon the seed coat fell away.
Big leaves grew on top.
My strong plant was on its way
To a fabulous bean crop!

My bean plant, you will agree,
Is a wondrous sight.
Part of it creeps underground
And part grows toward sunlight.

Soon I'll pick the lean green beans
That grow up slender poles.
I can't wait for Mom to make
Her green bean casserole!

Dictionary

Write a sentence using each vocabulary word.

contrary: opposite from what you expect

_____

_____

sprout: to begin to grow

_____

_____

stem: the part of a plant that holds it up

_____

_____

might: strength, power

_____

_____

wondrous: surprising, amazing

_____

_____

slender: tall and thin

_____

_____

Apply Vocabulary

Complete each sentence using a word from the word box.

Word Box		
contrary	might	slender
sprout	stem	wondrous

1. In just a few days, I saw a tiny tree _____ out of the ground.

2. She tried with all her _____ to pick up the heavy box.

3. A sunflower grows on a strong, sturdy _____.

4. Pine trees have _____ needles instead of wide leaves.

5. After it rained, I saw a _____ rainbow in the sky.

6. It seems _____, but Yuna is already taller than her older sister.

Write two new sentences. Use a word from the word box in each.

1. _____

_____

2. _____

_____

Answer Questions

Read and answer each question.

1. The narrator says that something sounds contrary. What contrary idea is the narrator referring to?

   Ⓐ The seed was sleeping and then woke up.

   Ⓑ The plant grew up and down.

   Ⓒ The roots were big and also small.

   Ⓓ The soil was dark and the sun was light.

2. The narrator describes the plant's "tiny fingers." What part of the plant does this refer to?

   Ⓐ the leaves

   Ⓑ the stem

   Ⓒ the vine

   Ⓓ the roots

3. The narrator knew the bean crop would be good when _____.

   Ⓐ the plant had big leaves on top

   Ⓑ the stem popped out of the soil

   Ⓒ the seed was planted in the ground

   Ⓓ the seed sprouted the first root

4. How does the narrator feel about growing bean plants?

   Ⓐ Growing a bean plant takes time and patience.

   Ⓑ It is fun to see how the plant points in two directions.

   Ⓒ Beans are easy to grow, and everyone should do it.

   Ⓓ Mom's green bean casserole is delicious.

5. How can you tell this poem is fiction?

   _____

   _____

   _____

6. Do you think the narrator enjoys gardening? Give evidence from the poem to support your answer.

   _____

   _____

Write About It

Graphic Organizer

Think about how the bean plant in the poem grows and changes. You will be asked to explain how a bean plant grows. Use the chart below to organize your writing.

	What happens?
First	
In a few days	
Then	
Finally	

Writing Prompt

On a separate sheet of paper, write a paragraph to explain how a bean plant grows. Use details from the poem.

Growing Up, Growing Strong

Topic: Growing Up, Growing Strong
Essential Question: What affects how we grow?

Tying It Together

Use the script below to guide students in discussing the essential question and what they have learned about the topic from the paired selections. Feel free to expand on these questions and responses.

To support visual learners, you may wish to cover up the sample responses and reproduce and distribute the discussion questions for students to refer to.

Questions	Sample Responses
What happens to all living things as they grow?	*They get bigger/taller and stronger.*
How do a plant's roots and a person's bones help each of them grow?	*Both roots and bones take in nutrients that a plant or person needs to grow.*
How does earth affect the growth of both plants and people?	*Plants start as a seed in the earth, and roots take in water and nutrients from the earth for the plant. People need Earth's gravity to make their bones and muscles strong enough to be healthy.*
What affects how living things grow?	*sunlight, gravity, food/nutrients like vitamin D and calcium, exercise (especially activities where you leave the ground, like jumping and climbing), water, soil/earth*
Which of these things affects both plants and people?	*sunlight, food/nutrients, water*
How was the topic "growing up, growing strong" shown in "Growing with Gravity"?	*It explained how sunlight, vitamin D, calcium, and gravity all work together to make bones grow long and muscles grow strong.*
How was the topic "growing up, growing strong" shown in "Lean Green Beans"?	*It described all the growth stages a bean plant goes through and what the plant needed.*
Why do you think these selections were paired together?	*They both talk about what makes things grow, but one is about people and the other is about plants. Also, they mention different kinds of growth, like strength and length.*

Plan Your Writing

Graphic Organizer

Think about the different ways that things grow in "Growing with Gravity" and "Lean Green Beans." You will be asked to explain what affects how people and plants grow. Use the chart below to organize your writing.

Growing with Gravity		
	stronger	**weaker**
What makes bones...		
What makes muscles...		

Lean Green Beans		
	up	**down**
What makes plants grow...		
The parts of the plants that grow...		

Write an Essay

Writing Prompt

Write an essay to explain how people grow and how plants grow. Give your essay a title. Include details from the selections. Use transitions to connect your ideas.

Title: _____

_____

_____

_____

_____

_____

_____

_____

_____

_____

_____

_____

_____

_____

_____

_____

Answer Key

TE = Teacher's Edition
SB = Student Book

The Value of Volunteering

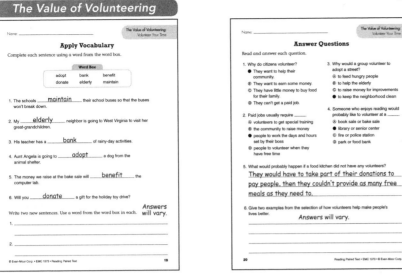

TE Page 19 / SB Page 5

Apply Vocabulary
Complete each sentence using a word from the word box.

Word Box: adopt, bank, benefit, donate, elderly, maintain

1. The schools __maintain__ their school buses so that the buses won't break down.
2. My __elderly__ neighbor is going to West Virginia to visit her great-grandchildren.
3. His teacher has a __bank__ of rainy-day activities.
4. Aunt Angela is going to __adopt__ a dog from the animal shelter.
5. The money we raise at the bake sale will __benefit__ the computer lab.
6. Will you __donate__ a gift for the holiday toy drive?

Write two new sentences. Use a word from the word box in each. *Answers will vary.*

TE Page 20 / SB Page 6

Answer Questions
Read and answer each question.

1. Why do citizens volunteer?
● They want to help their community.
○ They want to earn some money.
○ They have little money to buy food for their family.
○ They can't get a paid job.

2. Paid jobs usually require __.
● volunteers to get special training
○ the community to raise money
● people to work the days and hours set by their boss
○ people to volunteer when they have free time

3. Why would a group volunteer to adopt a street?
○ to feed hungry people
○ to help the elderly
○ to raise money for improvements
● to keep the neighborhood clean

4. Someone who enjoys reading would probably like to volunteer at a __.
○ book sale or bake sale
● library or senior center
○ fire or police station
○ park or food bank

5. What would probably happen if a food kitchen did not have any volunteers?
They would have to take part of their donations to pay people, then they couldn't provide as many free meals as they need to.

6. Give two examples from the selection of how volunteers help make people's lives better.
Answers will vary.

TE Page 27 / SB Page 11

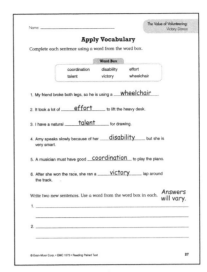

Apply Vocabulary
Complete each sentence using a word from the word box.

Word Box: coordination, disability, effort, talent, victory, wheelchair

1. My friend broke both legs, so he is using a __wheelchair__.
2. It took a lot of __effort__ to lift the heavy desk.
3. I have a natural __talent__ for drawing.
4. Amy speaks slowly because of her __disability__, but she is very smart.
5. A musician must have good __coordination__ to play the piano.
6. After she won the race, she ran a __victory__ lap around the track.

Write two new sentences. Use a word from the word box in each. *Answers will vary.*

TE Page 28 / SB Page 12

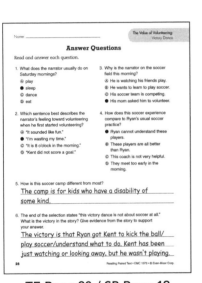

Answer Questions
Read and answer each question.

1. What does the narrator usually do on Saturday mornings?
Ⓐ play
● sleep
Ⓒ dance
Ⓓ eat

2. Which sentence best describes the narrator's feeling toward volunteering when he first started volunteering?
Ⓐ "It sounded like fun."
● "I'm wasting my time."
Ⓒ "It is 8 o'clock in the morning."
Ⓓ "Kent did not score a goal."

3. Why is the narrator on the soccer field this morning?
Ⓐ He is watching his friends play.
Ⓑ He wants to learn to play soccer.
Ⓒ His soccer team is competing.
● His mom asked him to volunteer.

4. How does this soccer experience compare to Ryan's usual soccer practice?
● Ryan cannot understand these players.
Ⓑ These players are all better than Ryan.
Ⓒ This coach is not very helpful.
Ⓓ They meet too early in the morning.

5. How is this soccer camp different from most?
The camp is for kids who have a disability of some kind.

6. The end of the selection states "this victory dance is not about soccer at all." What is the victory in the story? Give evidence from the story to support your answer.
The victory is that Ryan got Kent to kick the ball/ play soccer/understand what to do. Kent has been just watching or looking away, but he wasn't playing.

A Place to Call Home

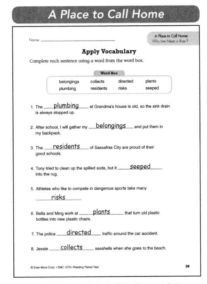

TE Page 39 / SB Page 21

Apply Vocabulary
Complete each sentence using a word from the word box.

Word Box: belongings, collects, directed, plants, plumbing, residents, risks, seeped

1. The __plumbing__ at Grandma's house is old, so the sink drain is always stopped up.
2. After school, I will gather my __belongings__ and put them in my backpack.
3. The __residents__ of Sassafras City are proud of their good schools.
4. Tony tried to clean up the spilled soda, but it __seeped__ into the rug.
5. Athletes who like to compete in dangerous sports take many __risks__.
6. Bella and Ming work at __plants__ that turn old plastic bottles into new plastic chairs.
7. The police __directed__ traffic around the car accident.
8. Jessie __collects__ seashells when she goes to the beach.

TE Page 40 / SB Page 22

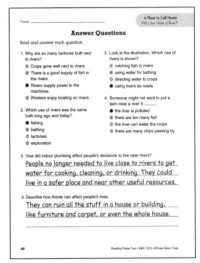

Answer Questions
Read and answer each question.

1. Why are so many factories built next to rivers?
○ Crops grow well next to rivers.
○ There is a good supply of fish in the rivers.
● Rivers supply power to the machines.
○ Workers enjoy boating on rivers.

2. Which use of rivers was the same both long ago and today?
● fishing
○ bathing
○ factories
○ exploration

3. Look at the illustration. Which use of rivers is shown?
○ catching fish in rivers
○ using water for bathing
● directing water to crops
○ using rivers as roads

4. Someone might not want to put a farm near a river if __.
● the river is polluted
○ there are too many fish
○ the river can water the crops
○ there are many ships passing by

5. How did indoor plumbing affect people's decisions to live near rivers?
People no longer needed to live close to rivers to get water for cooking, cleaning, or drinking. They could live in a safer place and near other useful resources.

6. Describe how floods can affect people's lives.
They can ruin all the stuff in a house or building, like furniture and carpet, or even the whole house.

TE Page 47 / SB Page 27

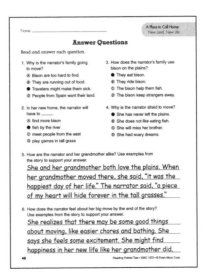

Apply Vocabulary
Complete each sentence using a word from the word box.

Word Box: community, declared, distance, elders, plentiful, rely, source

1. Our __elders__ have interesting stories to tell us about the past.
2. The library is a good __source__ for books and magazines.
3. Our neighborhood school offers art classes to the whole __community__.
4. There will be a __plentiful__ amount of blackberries this summer.
5. Baby snowy owls __rely__ on their parents to feed them.
6. The principal __declared__ today a snow day, so we got to stay home from school.
7. My home is a short __distance__ from the ball park.

Write two new sentences. Use a word from the word box in each. *Answers will vary.*

TE Page 48 / SB Page 28

Answer Questions
Read and answer each question.

1. Why is the narrator's family going to move?
Ⓐ Bison are too hard to find.
Ⓑ They are running out of food.
Ⓒ Travelers might make them sick.
● People from Spain want their land.

2. In her new home, the narrator will have to __.
Ⓐ find more bison
● fish by the river
Ⓒ meet people from the east
Ⓓ play games in tall grass

3. How does the narrator's family use bison on the plains?
● They eat bison.
Ⓑ They ride bison.
Ⓒ The bison help them fish.
Ⓓ The bison keep strangers away.

4. Why is the narrator afraid to move?
Ⓐ She has never left the plains.
Ⓑ She does not like eating fish.
Ⓒ She will miss her brother.
Ⓓ She had scary dreams.

5. How are the narrator and her grandmother alike? Use examples from the story to support your answer.
She and her grandmother both love the plains. When her grandmother moved there, she said, "it was the happiest day of her life." The narrator said, "a piece of my heart will hide forever in the tall grasses."

6. How does the narrator feel about her big move by the end of the story? Use examples from the story to support your answer.
She realizes that there may be some good things about moving, like easier chores and bathing. She says she feels some excitement. She might find happiness in her new life like her grandmother did.

Meeting the Father of a Country

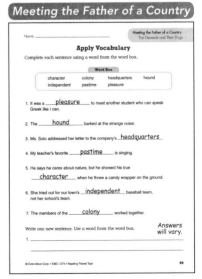

TE Page 59 / SB Page 37

Apply Vocabulary
Complete each sentence using a word from the word box.

Word Box: character, colony, headquarters, hound, independent, pastime, pleasure

1. It was a __pleasure__ to meet another student who can speak Greek like I can.
2. The __hound__ barked at the strange noise.
3. Ms. Soto addressed her letter to the company's __headquarters__.
4. My teacher's favorite __pastime__ is singing.
5. He says he cares about nature, but he showed his true __character__ when he threw a candy wrapper on the ground.
6. She tried out for our town's __independent__ baseball team, not her school's team.
7. The members of the __colony__ worked together.

Write one new sentence. Use a word from the word box. *Answers will vary.*

TE Page 60 / SB Page 38

TE Page 67 / SB Page 43

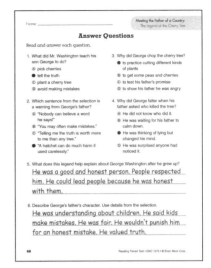

TE Page 68 / SB Page 44

Picturing the World

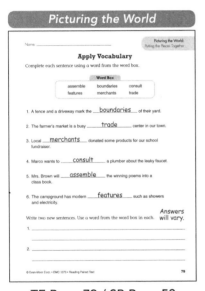

TE Page 79 / SB Page 53

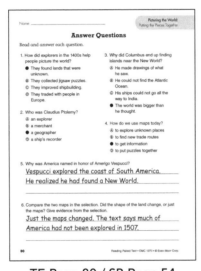

TE Page 80 / SB Page 54

TE Page 87 / SB Page 59

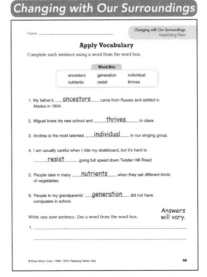

TE Page 88 / SB Page 60

Changing with Our Surroundings

TE Page 99 / SB Page 69

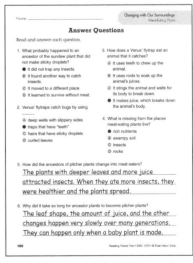

TE Page 100 / SB Page 70

TE Page 107 / SB Page 75

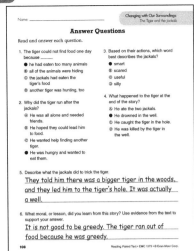

TE Page 108 / SB Page 76

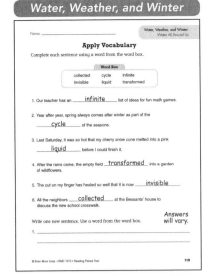

TE Page 119 / SB Page 85

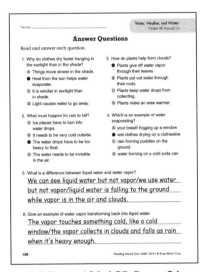

TE Page 120 / SB Page 86

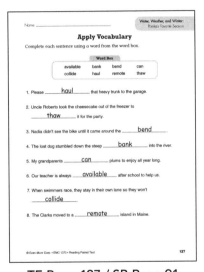

TE Page 127 / SB Page 91

TE Page 128 / SB Page 92

Observing Our World and Beyond

TE Page 139 / SB Page 101

TE Page 140 / SB Page 102

TE Page 147 / SB Page 107

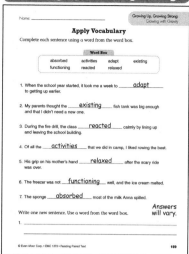

Observing Our World and Beyond: SpaceBook Friends

Answer Questions

Read and answer each question.

1. Which statement would the author agree with?
   Ⓐ Living on the ISS is very difficult.
   Ⓑ People cannot live in outer space for very long.
   Ⓒ Using a computer is the only way to learn things.
   ● You can learn by observing carefully.

2. Why does Rhea want to go to Earth?
   Ⓐ She misses her home planet.
   Ⓑ She wants to walk on ceilings and walls.
   ● She wants to try things that Diana enjoys.
   Ⓓ She wants to see how Earth and the ISS are similar.

3. Which of these is a difference between Rhea and Diana?
   Ⓐ Rhea always wears socks, and Diana never does.
   Ⓑ Rhea can see Diana, but Diana cannot see Rhea.
   ● Rhea is an alien, and Diana is a human being.
   Ⓓ Rhea lives indoors, but Diana is free to go outdoors.

4. Rhea wrinkled her forehead because she was ____.
   Ⓐ jealous
   ● puzzled
   Ⓒ excited
   Ⓓ upset

5. What events and details in the story tell you it is science fiction?
   Rhea's mother appearing on the wall, floating, having been born on the ISS, Titan and SpaceBook, headset camera, watch screen, gravity gym

6. Why do Rhea's feet rarely touch the floor of the ISS?
   There is no gravity on the ISS except in the gravity gym, so she mostly floats from place to place on the ISS.

148

Reading Paired Text • EMC 1373 • © Evan-Moor Corp.

TE Page 148 / SB Page 108

Growing Up, Growing Strong: Growing with Gravity

Apply Vocabulary

Complete each sentence using a word from the word box.

Word Box
absorbed	activities	adapt	existing
functioning	reacted	relaxed	

1. When the school year started, it took me a week to ___adapt___ to getting up earlier.

2. My parents thought the ___existing___ fish tank was big enough and that I didn't need a new one.

3. During the fire drill, the class ___reacted___ calmly by lining up and leaving the school building.

4. Of all the ___activities___ that we did in camp, I liked rowing the best.

5. His grip on his mother's hand ___relaxed___ after the scary ride was over.

6. The freezer was not ___functioning___ well, and the ice cream melted.

7. The sponge ___absorbed___ most of the milk Anna spilled.

Write one new sentence. Use a word from the word box.　　Answers will vary.

1. _____

© Evan-Moor Corp. • EMC 1373 • Reading Paired Text

159

TE Page 159 / SB Page 117

Growing Up, Growing Strong: Growing with Gravity

Answer Questions

Read and answer each question.

1. Someone who does not get much exercise will probably have ____.
   ● thinner bones
   Ⓑ more bones
   Ⓒ thicker bones
   Ⓓ fewer bones

2. How does gravity affect the heart?
   Ⓐ It makes the heart wear out sooner.
   ● It pushes blood from the heart to the head.
   Ⓒ It helps the heart more exercise.
   Ⓓ It helps the heart absorb more vitamin D.

3. Earth's gravity helps ____.
   Ⓐ give bones calcium
   ● make muscles strong
   Ⓒ get vitamin D from food
   Ⓓ make things easier to move

4. What should astronauts do to help their bones while they are in space?
   Ⓐ jump rope really fast
   Ⓑ climb the walls of the space station
   Ⓒ move heavy objects around
   ● use straps on an exercise machine

5. In some places in Earth's far north, the sun does not rise for over two months in winter. People who live in these areas can easily get thinner bones. Explain why, using details from the selection.
   Without sun, they don't get vitamin D, which means they don't absorb calcium from food. Without calcium, their bones can't get any thicker.

6. Give two reasons why changes happen to the bones of an astronaut who has been in space a long time.
   Bones get thin without gravity to react against. Without being in the sun, astronauts don't make vitamin D.

160

Reading Paired Text • EMC 1373 • © Evan-Moor Corp.

TE Page 160 / SB Page 118

Growing Up, Growing Strong: Jack Green Beans

Apply Vocabulary

Complete each sentence using a word from the word box.

Word Box
contrary	might	slender
sprout	stem	wondrous

1. In just a few days, I saw a tiny tree ___sprout___ out of the ground.

2. She tried with all her ___might___ to pick up the heavy box.

3. A sunflower grows on a strong, sturdy ___stem___.

4. Pine trees have ___slender___ needles instead of wide leaves.

5. After it rained, I saw a ___wondrous___ rainbow in the sky.

6. It seems ___contrary___, but Yuna is already taller than her older sister.

Write two new sentences. Use a word from the word box in each.　　Answers will vary.

1. _____

2. _____

© Evan-Moor Corp. • EMC 1373 • Reading Paired Text

167

TE Page 167 / SB Page 123

Growing Up, Growing Strong: Jack Green Beans

Answer Questions

Read and answer each question.

1. The narrator says that something sounds contrary. What contrary idea is the narrator referring to?
   Ⓐ The seed was sleeping and then woke up.
   ● The plant grew up and down.
   Ⓒ The roots were big and also small.
   Ⓓ The soil was dark and the sun was light.

2. The narrator describes the plant's "tiny fingers." What part of the plant does this refer to?
   Ⓐ the leaves
   Ⓑ the stem
   Ⓒ the vine
   ● the roots

3. The narrator knew the bean crop would be good when ____.
   ● the plant had big leaves on top
   Ⓑ the stem popped out of the soil
   Ⓒ the seed was planted in the ground
   Ⓓ the seed sprouted the first root

4. How does the narrator feel about growing bean plants?
   Ⓐ Growing a bean plant takes time and patience.
   ● It is fun to see how the plant points in two directions.
   Ⓒ Beans are easy to grow, and everyone should do it.
   Ⓓ Mom's green bean casserole is delicious.

5. How can you tell this poem is fiction?
   It has a narrator who plants the bean plant and will pick the beans. The narrator has a mother who makes green bean casserole.

6. Do you think the narrator enjoys gardening? Give evidence from the poem to support your answer.
   Yes, she really pays attention to how it grows; she uses the words "fabulous" and "wondrous sight."

168

Reading Paired Text • EMC 1373 • © Evan-Moor Corp.

TE Page 168 / SB Page 124